ALTERNATIVE COOKING

New ways; new ideas; new sensations:
a treasury of nutritious and
unusual recipes.

BY THE SAME AUTHOR
COOKING WITH FLOWERS

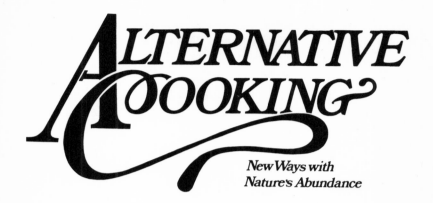

ALTERNATIVE COOKING

New Ways with Nature's Abundance

by

GREET BUCHNER

Translated from the Dutch by
Helena Brandt

THORSONS PUBLISHERS LIMITED
Wellingborough, Northamptonshire

Published in Holland as DE ALTERNATIEVE KEUKEN
© De Driehoek, Amsterdam
First published in England 1979

ISBN 0 7225 0514 0 (hardback)
ISBN 0 7225 0469 1 (paperback)

Printed and bound in Great Britain by
Weatherby Woolnough, Wellingborough,
Northants, England

Contents

Foreword

Among the young people of today lives the urgent wish to find new paths in almost every field. They look for and find new ways of living their lives. Therefore this book should satisfy the need in many people to start out on a healthier diet.

The ordinary science of nutrition looks upon foods as carbohydrates, proteins and fats. However, when we eat plants, eggs and drink milk, they give us far more than the total sum of their chemical ingredients. The most essential part is simply not mentioned, i.e. health.

If we are looking for healthy foods, it is of vital importance that we let ourselves be guided by the yearly rhythm, the seasons. We should use crops grown in our own moderate climate, when they are in season. We do this automatically when we use wild plants and fruits, but we shall have to learn to follow the same pattern when buying our vegetables.

The writer has very successfully created an immensely readable book. It is knowledgeable and inviting and will undoubtedly be used again and again, because of its many good ideas and excellent recipes.

H. E. Casparé
Retired Principal of Huis te Lande
(School of Home Economics)

Introduction

This 'cookery book with a difference' will offer the kind of recipes that cannot be found in ordinary everyday cookery-books. This cookery book is for people who are willing to walk new roads when they prepare their meals, because they know that everything one eats not only feeds the body, but influences the soul as well.

One of these roads leads us back to Nature. Especially in the spring and the summer months she has far more to offer than most people realize. Nature is generous. If she is not hampered by the spray-happy people of the seventies, she has much to offer. From the first tender leaves of the dandelion and the coltsfoot, to the full-flavoured tips of the stinging nettle or the elderberry.

In Autumn she surprises us with berries, mushrooms and even hazelnuts and sweet chestnuts.

This book will show you how to use the fresh green leaves, the scented flowers and the spicy berries. There are many different recipes, such as stewed coltsfoot or a healthy stinging-nettle hotchpotch.

Has it ever occurred to you, for instance, that the fragrant petals of a rose make a delicious jelly, or that the bright yellow flowers of the dandelion will make a tasty wine? Even the berries of the Mountain Ash can be made into a truly wonderful jelly, not to mention the endless possibilities of nuts and mushrooms. Why not go out and pick your own?

For those people who are unable to go out regularly and pick their meal by a stream, in the woods or the meadows, there are recipes of all kinds, including vegetables and fruit. It would be best, however, to use biodynamically grown produce only, in order to do the recipes justice. Biodynamically grown vegetables are not only free from all pesticides and fertilizers, apart from natural ones, but they also taste much better. In addition to the produce of Nature and the vegetables from the shop, every aspiring 'natural' cook should grow some herbs. If there is a garden available, so much the better. Even the tall lovage, the space-loving savory and dill may be grown. If there is only a windowsill, one should be satisfied with only parsley chives, garden cress, lemon balm and celery greens. They will go a long way and they grow well in pots behind the window-pane.

Not only green herbs and vegetables are mentioned in this book. Many old-fashioned grains and grain products are re-introduced and have been given a place of honour. Since the potato became our staple diet in the seventeenth century, grains have been gradually pushed out of our daily diet, and more is the pity. The use of grain products on a regular basis can help the business orientated human being of the twentieth century to recapture his emotional equilibrium. Moreover, some of these grain products, such as buckwheat, have qualities that can help prevent the hardening of the arteries and lessen the condition once it has started.

The most delicious dishes can be prepared with millet, unpolished rice and buckwheat, dishes that are as satisfying as they are healthy. It is not without reason that they play an important role in the macrobiotic kitchen, with its mysterious Yin and Yang theory.

In our western culture it is almost impossible to follow this principle to the word, but the macrobiotic idea has shown us the usefulness of sesame seed, sesame butter (tahina) and sesame oil (tamari), for which we should be grateful. Miso paste, made of sesame and sea salt, originated in the macrobiotic kitchen too. We happily make use of these products, as they not only heighten the taste of our food, but add so many vital mineral trace elements and protein to our daily diet as well.

This protein is a welcome alternative in our natural food programme, as no use is made of artificially bred animals that are killed for food only. Many people are convinced that we cannot live without the animal protein that meat provides. They are wrong!

The World Health Organisation (WHO) recommend a maximum intake of 50 grammes pure protein daily per person. (that is just under 2 oz.) The Dutch Food Consumer Advice Bureau, who are traditionally conservative in their statements, suggest 1 gramme per kilo of body-weight, averaging at 70 grammes per person.

Even if we keep this higher recommendation in mind, we can still easily get our daily 'requirement' without consuming animal protein. There is an abundance of vegetable protein available in Nature. Bread contains 8 per cent vegetable protein, grains in general contain some 10 per cent, and pulse and nuts, like meat, have a 20 per cent protein content.

A grain product, or half a loaf of wholemeal bread, supplemented with 100 grammes of pulses, some nuts and some lacto-protein provided by milk and dairy produce, will have supplied us with all the protein we need that day.

Most people, especially young people, who follow this dietary pattern feel livelier, are more cheerful and have more energy than before. Moreover, it enables them to be more creative in their jobs. This need surprise no one, when we come to realize that each cell in our bodies is built up out of the foodstuffs that we consume. If all our food has been refined and de-naturalized to such an extent that the trace elements are missing and most vitamins are gone, this must have an adverse effect on our health.

This is the main reason why we - of the alternative cuisine - are looking for natural foodstuffs and for additional products, such as the sesame range, that are still rich in mineral trace elements. Ordinary salt is replaced by sea salt, which contains as many as sixty different trace elements.

Refined and chemically prepared sugar is substituted by light-brown cane sugar that is still rich in iron and other trace elements. For cooking fats we use sunflower or maize oil, a pure vegetable margarine if necessary.

For flour we use exclusively freshly ground wholemeal flour, which contains every single part of the original grain, that danced in the sunshine to the rhythm of the wind.

1
Biodynamics

The biodynamic agricultural method is based on the philosophy of Rudolf Steiner, the founder of anthroposophy. According to the anthroposophical belief the kind and nature of a plant and its influence on the spiritual and physical well-being of Man are firmly linked together.

On a biodynamic farm grains, vegetables and fruit are grown by using natural organic fertilizers only and by sowing and harvesting at the most favourable time, which is partly determined by the position of moon and the stars. When and where possible the natural growing conditions are enhanced. Biodynamically grown produce is therefore free of all chemical poisons, will keep much longer, and tastes far better than any of the commercially grown and sprayed products. Biodynamic produce may not always look as good as its 'spray-cleaned' agricultural and horticultural counterparts, but it is, however, infinitely better.

It stands to reason that this cookery book presumes the use of unsprayed, preferably biodynamically grown vegetables and fruits. Even if we do use biodynamic foods only, it does not mean that we feed ourselves according to the anthroposophical diet theory.

This diet is based on the belief that there are four elements, which play an important part in the development of each living being, including plants. These four elements are earth, water, air and light (or warmth). In order to explain the idea in a simple manner, one could say that the roots of a plant are linked to earth and water. The stalks and leaves are linked to air and light, and the flowers and fruits are linked to light and warmth.

Should we look upon Man in a similar, and similarly simplified manner, we may come to the conclusion that the function of the human head (i.e., brain), which supervises, as it were, the intake of food and oxygen, could be compared to the function of the roots of a plant. The function of the chest (i.e., the lungs) is somewhat similar to the function of the stalks and leaves of a plant. The lower part of the body, with its excretory and procreative organs, might be compared with the flowering and fruit-bearing functions of the plant.

Rudolf Steiner goes further still, and says that the identical functions of human beings and plants may be used to help one another. For instance, the eating of roots and bulbous vegetables in the early years of development of a child is said to influence the nervous and sense organs, as well as the growth towards materialism and egoism. Stalks and leaves benefit the rhythmic processes of breathing and blood circulation. Fruit and seeds aid the digestive system, as well as the emotional urge to act. Seen in this light, one should not underestimate the influence of vegetable foods on people of all four human temperaments, which are in turn linked closely to the four elements.

According to this theory a melancholy (i.e., earth-bound) person should eat grains and fruits. The sanguine person with his carefree soul should add roots and bulbs to his daily diet. The short-tempered choleric person would benefit if he ate quantities of stalks and roots each day, while the slow and phlegmatic person should look for the fire element in his food, such as the spicy, aromatic onions, the radish, mustard and herbs like rosemary and thyme.

2
Macrobiotics

The teaching of macrobiotics — and we are talking of the real thing, not everything that goes by that name — is based on Zen Buddhism and originated in the Far East. Diet forms an important part of the philosophy of Zen Buddhism, which is based on the universal principle of opposite forces that must be kept in perfect balance. These forces are called Yin, being the centrifugal force and Yang, the centripetal force. Though opposites they are inseparable and complement each other, like man and woman, day and night, saline and acid. These forces are active in each person, and should the balance between the forces be disturbed, illness may follow.

What is Yin and what is Yang?

Yin is: female, blue, green, cold, wet, acid, dark, passive, negative and vertical.

Yang is: male, red, yellow and orange, warm, dry, saline, light, active, bitter, positive and horizontal.

The shape of a plant will mostly tell us whether a plant is Yin or Yang in character. Yin plants can be recognized by their under-developed roots, the tall stalks and juice fruit. Yang plants have an impressive root system, few stalks and leaves and small yellow or red fruit.

Fortunately for us, macrobiotics is not entirely dependent on Nature for its Yin and Yang foods. The method of preparation can heighten the Yin or Yang character of a plant.

The use of much water, when boiling a vegetable, and the addition of vinegar, lemon and sugar intensifies the Yin force. Roasting, frying (with little oil) and the use of salt and bitter herbs strengthens the Yang character of a plant.

In a well-planned macrobiotic diet Yin and Yang foods are kept in perfect balance, though this does not imply that the actual composition of the diet is always the same.

Some macrobiotic diets will consist of 100 per cent grains and grain products. Others contain 60 per cent grains, 25 per cent fruit and vegetables and 15 per cent animal foodstuffs. In between these two are many variations. A common factor in all macrobiotic diets is the use of a maximum of locally grown products and the rejection of all preserved foods.

The nightshade family, to which our potato, the tomato and spanish pepper belong, are not held in high esteem in the macrobiotic kitchen. However, grains play a major part and much attention is paid to wild plants, like the dandelion, the stinging nettle and others.

All vegetable dishes should be kept as crisp as possible, as overcooked vegetables might be swallowed without chewing. Chewing is very important, as it helps the digestive system to make the most of our food. Each bite should be chewed approximately fifty times, but that is only feasible for fully-fledged followers of macrobiotics.

Sea Salt

It may seem strange to pay extra attention to salt, but it fits in the framework of alternate cookery.

The chemical structure of sea salt is totally different from ordinary refined salt. Kitchen salt is practically pure sodium chloride. Though sea salt also consists of sodium chloride, in addition it contains many trace elements, which are vital for our bodies' well-being. To mention just a few: potassium, calcium, magnesium, zinc, manganese, bromine, iodine. There are literally only traces of these minerals to be found in sea salt, but they are essential in a well-balanced diet. However, sea salt, like ordinary kitchen salt, should always be used sparingly. Sodium chloride is not good for health.

Unfortunately, we have grown so used to the taste of salt in our food that we no longer enjoy our meals, if the salt is missing. But we can try to walk the middle road between eating good salt-free and an excessive use of salt.

3

Wild and Cultivated Vegetables

This chapter offers a great variety of wild vegetable recipes, very tempting, but not entirely without dangers. Most people will have little difficulty in recognizing a stinging nettle or a dandelion, but when it comes to picking coltsfoot, orache and Good King Henry problems may arise. This proves the point that the picking of herbs and vegetables in the wild should only be done by people with a knowledge of plants, or accidents might happen. Even an extensive knowledge of our flora will not be enough, however, when no attention is payed to man-made poisoning, on gathering a meal from the fields. Newly-sprayed greens are lethal, and greens that grow within a hundred yards from a motorway will at the very least contain a dangerous quantity of lead. A natural meal that includes lead-poisoning cannot possibly be anyone's intention.

Picking berries and mushrooms in Autumn is a rewarding job, but care should be taken at all times.

The recipes of the wild crops are only aimed at those people who have a chance to pick some of Nature's bounty.

For the botanists among readers it might be of interest to know that there are many edible plants in addition to the ones mentioned in this book. To mention just a few: the young shoots of Good King Henry (CHENOPODIUM BONUS HENRICUS) make a lovely stewed vegetable dish, as does marsh samphire (SALICORNIA HERBACEA). The latter should be left to soak in water for approximately one hour to extract some of its salt.

The young leaves of the yarrow or milfoil (ACHILLEA MILLEFOLIUM) and the common garden daisy (BELLIS PERENNIS) are not eaten as a vegetable, but are very useful as condiments in soups or salads. A handful of daisies sprinkled on salad may seem a little cruel, but it tastes surprisingly nice.

Plantain (PLANTAGO) in both its broad- and narrow-leaved varieties, is very tasty, as is ground ivy (GLECHOMA HEDERACEA), which belongs to the family of thyme and rosemary.

Scurvy grass (COCHLEARIA) used to be quite popular with our great-grandmothers, which is hardly surprising as it is closely related to the cabbage family.

Speedwell (VERONICA) was also often used in salads. In short there is plenty of variety and endless possibility when looking for food in the meadow; BUT: care should be taken at all times.

Concerning commercially grown herbs and vegetables, we should only use the vegetables that are in season, e.g., runner beans in summer and cabbage in winter.

Vegetables that are on sale out of season are usually artificially grown under glass, pampered and artfully kept fresh. Their quality can never compare with a healthy green that is eaten straight after harvesting. At all times biodynamically grown vegetables are preferred, or at least un-sprayed ones.

As the preparation of most commercial vegetables is common knowledge to most people, there are only a few unusual recipes given, mainly of soups.

For those people who would like to cook their vegetables with a little extra care, we give, briefly, the healthiest ways of cooking vegetables.

1. Steaming in a colander over boiling water. Especially suitable for leaf vegetables.
2. Quick frying in a little oil, so that the vegetables remain crisp.
3. Stewing, i.e., short frying in a little oil, adding a little water, covering and leaving to cook.
4. Boiling, the most common and old-fashioned way of preparing vegetables, which can be used for all varieties. Put

hard vegetables in cold water and bring to the boil, but soft vegetables should go straight into boiling water.

5. Baking in the oven on a slightly-oiled baking tray. Especially suitable and successful with various root vegetables.

Stinging Nettle

The large perennial stinging nettle is a true friend, and can be easily found, for it grows everywhere from early Spring to late Autumn. Stinging nettles have depurative qualities, are full of vitamins and form an indispensable addition to our daily diet.

We pick them from early spring onwards, using gloves to protect against the stinging, and a pair of scissors. We only pick the tender light-green tips, because they taste best and contain most vitamins.

We never pick more than we need, as stinging nettles are common and we can always go back for more the next day.

Boiled Stinging Nettle

Pick as much as you need for your family. Wash the nettles carefully and cook them — like spinach — with little or no water. Serve as soon as they are done — no more than seven minutes — with a little sesame oil, some toasted sesame seed or a little salad cream. Make use of the vegetable water as well. It makes a nice tea and works wonders as a cold-remedy.

The vegetable-water may also be used as a hair-rinse. It leaves the hair healthy and shiny and gives it body. In short, the lowly stinging nettle can be used for many things and in many ways.

Stinging Nettle Soup

The tenderest tips of the stinging nettle are kept for the soup. We wash them and dip them in hot water, to take out the 'sting'.

Chop them up very finely and add them to a vegetable soup, a creamed white soup or a potato soup. It tastes delicious and it is, undoubtedly, the best remedy against spring fatigue.

A clear CONSOMMÉ can be turned into an exciting spicy soup by adding a handful of chopped stinging nettles.

Stinging Nettle Hotchpotch

Pick only the tender tips of the stinging nettle for this lovely hotchpotch that gives strength and vitality. We need approximately

400 grammes (14 oz.) or at least a small basketful.

Boil 1 kilogram (2¼ lb) of potatoes and mash them with milk, a knob of butter and a pinch of nutmeg.

Wash the nettles, chop them up finely and mix them into the mashed potatoes. Heat thoroughly and serve with fried onion-rings.

Stewed Coltsfoot

During the first days of spring, sometimes as early as the beginning of March, a small yellow flower, somewhat similar to the dandelion flower, can be found by the roadside and under shrubs. A few weeks later the leaves will follow — quite a large, slightly hairy leaf. This is what we have been waiting for.

Pick enough of the coltsfoot leaves for a meal, wash them thoroughly, but do not break them. Carefully arrange them in a pan and add a little water. Cook these spicy aromatic leaves in approximately seven minutes. Strain — and use the water for a soup or a sauce.

Place the cooked coltsfoot leaves on a pre-heated dish and cover them with breadcrumbs toasted in oil.

Serve with potatoes and a hard-boiled egg, if desired. It makes a tasty spring meal.

Sorrel with Raisins

In May sorrel is at its best. However, it can and should be picked and eaten during every one of the following summer months. Sorrel is delicious and can be made into a number of lovely dishes.

Do not pick more than is needed for one meal at the time, but pick generously for Nature is not frugal and children love the sour taste of sorrel — especially when sorrel is prepared with raisins.

Wash the sorrel carefully, pluck the leaves off the stalks and chop them up finely.

Put a tablespoonful of sunflower oil in a heavy pan, add the chopped sorrel and cook over a low fire. Add a generous handful of raisins during the stewing. The raisins should have been pre-soaked for a couple of hours.

Add one or two spoonsful of honey or brown sugar, according to taste, and thicken, if necessary, with a little cornflour. Serve with mashed potatoes, it is destined to become a great family favourite.

Herb Salt

A jar of herb salt made with fresh garden herbs is an essential addition to winter dishes and so easy to make.

Needed are:

25g (1 oz.) parsley
25g (1 oz.) chives
25g (1 oz.) dill
25g (1 oz.) lovage

The freshly cut herbs are washed, dried and chopped up very finely. They are placed in a stone or glass jar in layers alternating sea salt and the herb mixture. The top layer must be salt, of course. When the jar is full it must be made airtight and stored in a dark, cool place. After approximately three weeks the herb salt is ready for use. Provided it is kept in a cool place, it should stay fresh and aromatic until the next spring.

Sorrel and Spinach

Should you have any sorrel left, simply mix it with spinach the next day. Cook and chop them up together. Strange as it may sound, the spinach becomes milder in taste, gentler as it were, when it is cooked with a few leaves of fresh sorrel.

Sorrel and Ginger

Wash the sorrel, chop up the leaves and stew them in a little sunflower oil till they are done.

Add a teaspoonful of ginger powder, or a little fresh ginger, and a teaspoonful of finely chopped onions after a few minutes.

When done, thicken with breadcrumbs (just like spinach) and a dash of cream. Eggs go well with gingered sorrel. Unpolished rice and a bean sauce are a good combination as well.

Cream of Sorrel Soup with Egg

250g (9 oz.) sorrel
1 litre (1¾ pt.) vegetable broth
5 tablespoonsful flour
2½ tablespoonsful oil
sea salt
milk or cream

Wash the sorrel and cook in very little water.

When boiled down, add the vegetable broth. Boil for approximately five minutes and strain.

Meanwhile, in a large saucepan, make a Hollandaise sauce with the oil and the flour. Stirring all the time, the sorrel and vegetable broth is gradually added.

Simmer for a few minutes, season and add the milk or cream, taking the saucepan off the heat.

Just before serving, chopped up hard-boiled egg or thin strips of omelette are sprinkled in the soup. Serve with wholemeal toast.

A few pancakes or a generous serving of buckwheat porridge will complete the meal.

Cream of Potato Soup with Sorrel

1 litre (1¾ pt.) vegetable broth
500g (18 oz.) potatoes
250g (9 oz.) sorrel
1 head of butter lettuce
1 large onion
1 tablespoonful margarine
1 tablespoonful flour
salt, pepper
1 carton of thick yogurt
1 egg yolk

Cook the finely-chopped sorrel and lettuce leaves in the vegetable broth. Boil the potatoes, strain them and pass them through a sieve, or mash. Fry a finely-chopped onion slightly brown in the margarine, add the flour and finally, stirring all the time, add the broth with the green vegetables as well as the sieved potatoes. Bring to the boil once more.

Meanwhile, mix the yogurt and the egg yolk and divide the mixture over four soup plates.

Pour the boiling-hot soup over the mixture into the plates.

Chickweed Salad

From early spring onwards chickweed is a common sight to gardeners. This fragile plant with its small leaves and lovely white star-shaped flowers will grow on every available open spot.

It is always there, so next time the gardens need weeding, don't throw away the chickweed. Keep it, wash it carefully, chop it up a little and make it into a delightful salad.

It only needs a dressing of oil, vinegar and a little sea salt, which should be poured on just before serving as chickweed is delicate and will spoil by standing.

Chickweed Hotchpotch

Mash potatoes with milk and a knob of butter. Season with a little pepper and some sea salt, but do not add any nutmeg or other strong spices and herbs. Shortly before serving, mix the well-washed, chopped up chickweed through the mashed potatoes and top this refreshing spring meal with grated mature cheese.

Nasturtium Capers

The seeds of the nasturtium can easily be made into mock-capers. They can be used as ordinary capers to decorate cold buffet dishes and on salads. Provided they are made the right way, they can be kept for years. Pick the nasturtium seeds when they are approximately one week old, i.e., one week after the flower has wilted and dropped off. Do not wait longer or the seeds will grow too large.

Fill an earthenware jar with alternate layers of the seeds and some bay leaves, dill and if possible a few slices of fresh horse radish. Boil a little wine vinegar with a shallot, 20g (1 oz.) of sea salt and a few peppercorns. Leave to simmer for ten minutes and allow to cool. Pour the cooled vinegar over the nasturtium seeds until they are completely covered.

Cover the jar with aluminium foil and leave it in a cool place. It will take a few weeks before the 'capers' are ready for use.

Nasturtium Salad

Pick the young leaves of the nasturtium, without the stems. Wash these beautiful round leaves and mix them with ordinary butter lettuce into a refreshing green salad. It looks best if the nasturtium leaves are left intact, but they may be chopped up.

Place a single nasturtium flower on the salad for decoration.

Strange though it may sound, these bright flowers taste very good, too, but it may take a moments' hesitation before one can put so brilliant a splash of colour into one's mouth.

Dandelion

From April onwards the dandelion grows new leaves again and they are not hard to find, for wherever there is grass there are dandelions, even in the lawn! The tastiest, tenderest dandelion leaves are found on mole hills. It used to be called mole lettuce.

If you cannot find any mole hills, do not despair. Ordinary, freshly picked leaves taste good too.

When picking dandelion leaves care should be taken that the chosen verge of the road has not recently been sprayed with a weed killer by spray-happy council workers. It should usually be quite apparent the day after, as all vegetation turns brown and dry, but do make sure before picking a meal.

Pick as many crisp, fresh green leaves as can be found during the walk, as they can be used in many different ways.

Pick a few of the gold-coloured flowers, as well, as they can be made into a delightfully refreshing wine.

At home the leaves need sorting. The smallest light-green leaves, preferably even a little bleached because the tall grass has hidden them from the light, are kept for a salad. The stronger leaves are cooked as a spring vegetable and the flowers are kept for making wine.

Dandelion Salad

Wash the young leaves and stems very carefully, as they are likely to be covered in sand. Cut them into fine strips and soak them in water for one hour to take out some of the bitterness.

Make a dressing of:

4 tablespoonsful oil
4 teaspoonsful lemon-juice
1 teaspoonful finely chopped chives

Pour the dressing over the dandelion and toss the mix thoroughly. This salad, which is very rich in Vitamin C and iron, has a delicious flavour, though slightly bitter.

Children do not usually like it, unless their individual serving is sweetened with brown sugar or a spoonful of toasted sesame seeds.

Stewed Dandelion Leaves

The firm green leaves left over after the salad making, are also washed but left whole. Arrange them carefully, shoulder to shoulder, as it were, in a heavy saucepan. Add a little boiling water, cover and leave to simmer for approximately fifteen minutes or until done.

Scoop them out of the water, drain them well and arrange them neatly onto a heated dish. Pour a quick cream-cheese sauce, or an ordinary Hollandaise sauce with some nuts over the vegetable.

Served with an omelette and boiled potatoes, it makes a lovely spring meal packed with vitamins and mineral trace elements.

Dandelion Wine

Now we have only the dandelion flowers left from our harvesting-walk. Measure them in a measuring cup, as we need the same quantity of water. For two litres (3½ pt.) of yellow flower heads we need:

2 litres (3½ pt.) water
750g (26 oz.) honey
2 sliced lemons
10g (½ oz.) yeast

Place the flowers in a large stoneware jar, pour on the water and cover. Make certain that only the flowers and no pieces of stems or leaves are in the jar.

Cover the jar with a lid and leave it at room temperature for at least one week. Pass the flowers through a sieve until the last drop of fluid has been extracted. Mix this aromatic juice with the honey, the sliced lemons, and the yeast and pour the mixture back into the jar. Replace the lid and leave it once again for a week or so.

Pour the mixture through a strainer and once more into the jar. Leave it until it has stopped fermenting.

Now comes the fun of bottling the wine. Choose small bottles, e.g., beer bottles. Clean them well with soda water, pour in the delicious drink and put in the corks.

Leave the bottles for a few more weeks before sampling the first of the dandelion wine.

Roses

Whoever has heard of eating roses? The most splendid and colourful flower that June has to offer. One wouldn't dream of picking them for eating, or would one? Why not? Why not experiment with the sweet, fragrant rose?

Rose honey would be a good start. It's hard to imagine a more romantic or fragrant honey to decorate the breakfast table or heighten the pleasure of teatime.

Pick a few roses of unsprayed rose bushes. Preferably pick red roses as the dark colour makes the honey look better.

Remove the narrow white lower part of the petals by which they are attached to the receptacle. Heat a jar of honey and add a cupful of chopped-up red rose petals.

Heat the mixture thoroughly, but do not let it come to the boil. Pour the rose-honey into an ovenproof dish and leave it in a cool place, though not in the refrigerator which is too cold.

Heat once more, very slowly in the ovenware dish over very low heat, taking care never to let it come to boiling point. Strain and pour the honey into clean jam jars. Use it at breakfast on toast, at -teatime in sandwiches or to sweeten porridge or muesli. The taste is enthralling.

Save a few jars for the winter months, as the taste and the fragrance of roses will then be appreciated even more.

Rose Syrup

Pick as many red rose petals as you can find in June when the roses are most fragrant.

Remove the lower white parts and alternately pour hot and cold water over the petals. This should be repeated twenty times altogether, or until the petals are brittle and fragile. Weigh them and mix them with an equal quantity of sugar. Add a generous measure of lemon juice and bring the mixture to the boil. Leave it to boil down to a syrupy consistency. Leave to cool slightly and pour the warm syrup into clean jars. Cover the jars when the syrup has cooled.

Rosehip Jam

Towards the end of September is the time to start looking for ripe rosehips. Make certain that only unsprayed bushes are selected and only ripe hips are picked.

Wash the rosehips carefully and try to remove the pips.

There are two ways of doing this: either bring the hips briefly to the boil and pass them through a sieve (This method is easy, but wasteful); or, bring the fruit to the boil, scoop out of the water, cut the rosehips in half and empty them of as many pips as possible with a teaspoon. Chop up the halves and pass them through the sieve.

Mix the rosehip paste with a third of its own quantity in honey. Pour the mixture into a preserving jar and cook 'au bain Marie' for fifteen minutes, i.e., place the jar in a saucepanful of water, bring the water to the boil and keep it boiling gently.

Store this jam in a cool place. It is so rich in vitamin C that a teaspoonful a day will remedy any vitamin C deficiency during the winter.

Jam of Uncooked Rosehips

Wait until the frost has gone over the rosehips a few times, for it will prepare them for this delicious jam.

Pick the rosehips, wash them, cut them in half and remove the pips. Chop them up and mix them with an equal quantity of sugar. Stir and keep stirring for at least thirty minutes — the whole family can take a turn!

This jam should, under no circumstance, be heated, as this would spoil its qualities. Keep the jam in well-cleaned jars in a cool, dry place.

A teaspoonful a day will suffice to keep up the vitamin C level of a normal, balanced diet during the winter months.

Rose Jelly

50 dark-red fragrant roses
1 litre (1¾ pt.) boiled and cooled water
150g (5 oz.) sugar
lemon juice to taste
a knob of butter

Boil the sugar and the water down to a syrup. Add the lemon juice and the rose petals, of which the white lower parts have been removed. Add a knob of butter to clarify the mixture and bring it to the boil. Keep gently boiling for one hour, stirring all the time. The family can help! The stirring is very important in order to preserve the colour of the rose petals.

Pour into well-cleaned jars and cover, when the jelly has cooled and set.

Rose Honey

250g (9 oz.) red rose petals
2kg (4½ lb) honey
1½ litres (2¼ pt.) water

Remove the hard, white ends of the rose petals and place them in a stoneware jar. Pour the boiling water over the petals, stir well and leave in a cool place for twelve hours.

Strain and pass the petals through a sieve, preferably made of horse-hair as this will preserve the colour better.

Add this rose-water to the 2kg of honey and boil down the mixture to normal honey consistency over a low fire.

Fill jam jars and cover them when the rose honey has cooled.

Crystalized Rose Petals

This is no more than an extravagance, meant to turn an ordinary dessert into a luxury.

Pick pink rose petals, wash them, remove the white lower part and allow them to dry thoroughly. Carefully paint each petal with loosely beaten egg white and cover it with sugar. Repeat the whole procedure once.

Arrange the sugared petals on a baking sheet covered with aluminium foil. Allow them to dry quickly in the sun — or a lukewarm oven with the oven door slightly open and turn them over regularly.

When the petals have dried thoroughly and feel crisp to the touch they are placed gently in a tin, layered between sheets of grease-proof paper.

Close the tin airtight. Decorate puddings, cakes and little sweets with them. The effect will be even more stunning if a few crystalized violets are added as well.

Tea of Rosehip Pips

The pips that are left over from the preparation of the rosehip jam are not thrown away. They are toasted gently to remove the fine hair and then they are thoroughly cleaned.

When cool, they are stored in an airtight tin. Make tea in the ordinary way and serve it with honey and lemon juice.

It is said to sooth the nerves.

Crystalized Sweet Violets or Borage Flowers

500g (1 lb) sugar
1 cupful water
1 cupful sweet violets or borage flowers

Bring the sugar and the water to the boil and have the cooking thermometer ready.

As soon as the temperature of the syrup reaches 115°C (239°F), a dozen flowers are lowered into the boiling syrup. Scoop them out after one minute and put them onto a baking sheet covered with aluminium foil. Repeat until all the flowers have been coated with sugar syrup.

Place the baking sheet into a very low oven — or in the sun — so that the flowers can dry. When the top looks dry, they should be turned over once. Handle them with great care as they are extremely fragile.

The crystalized flowers are stored — like the rose petals — between layers of kitchen paper in airtight tins.

Sweet Violet Sugar

It may be heartbreaking to extract the juice of the beautiful, fragrant dark-purple flowers of the sweet violet, but if you do, you will be amply rewarded with a delicious, aromatic sugar, which can be used for making fudge or marzipan.

Pass the washed sweet violets through a very fine sieve and stir in as much sugar as the violet juice will take.

Spread the mixture onto a baking sheet and let it dry thoroughly in a lukewarm oven. Store it in an airtight jar.

Elder

The elder blossoms around Midsummer's Night (21 June) and both its blossoms and the dark-eyed berries, which follow later in the year, can be eaten and enjoyed.

Elder Blossom Fritters

The delicately scented elder blossoms can be made into a delicious dessert.

Pick one large umbel of blossom per person. Make a batter of two eggs, a little lukewarm milk and some wholemeal flour. Gently wash the umbels, drain them well and dip them into the batter. Deep fry them in hot oil until they are golden-brown and crisp.

Serve them hot, sprinkled with sugar or pour a little warmed honey over the top.

Elderberry Jam

Pick fresh ripe elderberries, wash them and strip them off the umbels. Mix them with an equal quantity of sugar. Add the grated peel and the juice of two lemons and slowly, over very low heat, boil this mixture down to the required thickness.

Pour the hot jam into well-cleaned jars. Cover them when the jam has cooled and store them in a cool place.

Yogurt Soup with Cucumber

To make a change from all the hot soup recipes, here is one for a delicious cold soup. A welcome starter on a very hot summer night.

1 litre (1¾ pt.) yogurt
1 large cucumber
2 tablespoonsful oil
1 clove garlic
½ cupful grated walnut
salt

Grate the cucumber on a coarse grater. Mix it with the oil, the salt, the very finely-chopped clove of garlic and finally add the yogurt.

Divide the mixture into four soup bowls, stir in a little boiled, cooled water if the soup is too thick.

Chill thoroughly. Sprinkle the walnuts on top just before serving.

Red Sweet Pepper and Paprika Soup

This soup of Hungarian origin not only looks red, but makes one feel red hot as well, thanks to the spicy paprika.

1 litre (1¾ pt.) clear vegetable broth
3 sweet peppers (preferably red)
2 onions
5 tomatoes
3 tablespoonsful margarine or sunflower oil
1 tablespoonful sweet paprika powder
2 tablespoonsful cooked rice
salt
1 carton thick yogurt

Wash and clean the peppers, removing the seeds. Cut them into thin strips and gently fry them with the finely chopped onion in the margarine or oil. Add the paprika powder, the peeled and cut up tomatoes and last, but not least the vegetable broth.

Leave the soup to simmer for half an hour, add the cooked rice and season to taste. The yogurt is added just before serving, as it should only be heated, but never be allowed to boil.

Serve with finely-chopped parsley or chives.

Celery and Mint Soup

1 litre (1¾ pt.) vegetable broth or water and marmite
3 large sprigs of celery-greens
1 sprig of fresh garden-mint
1 large onion
1 tablespoonful oil
2 tablespoonsful flour
2 tablespoonsful milk

Chop the washed celery greens, the mint and the onion finely, and fry gently in the oil until soft, but not brown. Add the flour and brown slightly, not too dark, though, as this will spoil the delicate flavour of the herbs. Remove the saucepan from the heat and whisk in the hot vegetable broth and the milk. Bring quickly back to the boil, season with sea salt and sprinkle a little fresh celery green on top just before serving.

Dutch Runner Bean Soup

1 litre (1¾ pt.) vegetable broth
200g. (7 oz.) runner beans
1 onion
1 large slice of celeriac
2 tablespoonsful sunflower oil
2 tablespoonsful cooked rice
½ cupful tomato purée

Cook the washed and chopped runner beans in the broth until they are done. Scoop them out, drain them and fry them with the chopped onion and the chopped celeriac in the oil. Add the broth again, as well as the cooked rice and the tomato purée. Simmer the soup for approximately ten minutes and serve it with small strips of fried bread ('soldiers').

Shepherd's Purse Soup

Everyone knows the shepherd's purse with its small green and white flowers and its elegant heart-shaped seed-pods.

Why not pick a good serving of the fresh green leaves of this plant, that belongs to the cabbage family? Pick a handful of stinging nettle tips as well, and make it into a soup:

3 onions
2 cupsful chopped shepherd's purse and stinging nettle leaves
1 cupful chopped parsley, celery greens, chervil and chives.

Fry one of the onions in a little oil until it is soft.

Add the other two finely-chopped onions and the fresh herbs. Add water and simmer the soup over very low heat for approximately one hour. Sprinkle some fresh herbs on the soup just before serving and season with marmite, if desired.

Fennel in Vegetable Broth

3 fennel roots
½ litre (¾ pt.) vegetable broth
salt and pepper to taste
3 tablespoonsful breadcrumbs

3 tablespoonsful grated cheese
2 tablespoonsful sunflower oil

Wash the fennel, scrape the outside clean and cut off the fine green sprigs. Keep them and use them in soups or sauces.

Cut the fennel into finger-thick slices and place them into the boiling vegetable broth. Cook for approximately twenty minutes or until they are done. Scoop them gently out of the broth and carefully arrange them in a buttered ovenware dish. Mix the breadcrumbs and the grated cheese and sprinkle the mixture over the fennel. Finally sprinkle the oil over the top. Place the dish in a warm oven and heat thoroughly for about fifteen minutes, or until golden brown. Serve with dry boiled rice, wheat or buckwheat. Mashed potatoes taste well with it, too.

Salsify Soup

1 litre (1¾ pt.) vegetable broth
250g (9 oz.) salsify
50g (2 oz.) margarine
4 large potatoes
nutmeg, salt and pepper
3 tablespoonsful sour cream

Place the salsify in boiling water. When it has cooled, it is quite easy to remove the outer skin.

Cut the clean, skinned salsify into lengths of 2cm (just under an inch) and fry them in the margarine until slightly brown. Add nutmeg, salt and pepper to taste. Grate the potatoes coarsely and add them, together with the vegetable broth, to the fried salsify. Bring the soup to the boil and simmer until the salsify is done. Stir in the sour cream just before serving. Chopped chives adds an extra flavour to this lovely soup.

White Cabbage and Potato Soup
A delicious winter soup that is warm and satisfying.

1 litre (1¾ pt.) vegetable broth
½ white cabbage
75g (3 oz.) margarine

2 teaspoonsful sweet paprika powder
1 apple
1 potato
cumin seed
a mixture of 4 tablespoonsful milk and 2 tablespoonsful
flour
salt, pepper and a little marjoram to taste.

Cut up the cabbage into very small pieces and fry them gently with the cumin seed in the margarine, till the cabbage is soft but not brown. Add the chopped-up apple and the potato, the paprika powder and the broth. Cover and gently simmer, until the potato is done. Cream the soup with the mixture of milk and flour. Season with salt, pepper and a pinch of marjoram to taste.

Carrot Soup

1 litre (1¾ pt.) vegetable broth
200g (7 oz.) winter carrots
2 onions
1 tablespoonful oil
1 tablespoonful flour
5 tablespoonsful milk
500g (18 oz.) grated cheese
parsley, chervil or chives

Wash and peel the carrots. Grate half of them, cut the other half into matchstick strips.

Chop the onion finely and gently fry in a little margarine until it is soft and golden-brown. Add the carrots and the vegetable broth, cover and simmer gently until the carrots are done.

Heat the oil, add the flour and gradually add the milk, stirring vigorously all the time. Gradually add the carrot broth, making it into a beautiful creamed soup. Sprinkle the cheese into the soup, heat it for just a moment until the cheese has melted. Sprinkle the finely-chopped green herbs on top.

Served with wholemeal bread or rye bread, this soup will make a meal for four people.

Polish Beetroot Soup

1 litre (1¾ pt.) vegetable broth
3 uncooked beetroots
bay leaves, cumin seed, salt and pepper
1 tablespoonful vinegar
50g (2 oz.) flour
1/8 litre (¼ pt.) fresh cream
Peel and grate the beetroots on a coarse grater. Cook them with
the spices and the vinegar in the broth until they are done.
  Thicken the soup with a mixture of the cream and the flour, bring
to the boil and serve very hot.

Stuffed Beetroots
A great favourite, that originated in the biodynamic kitchen, which
always keeps in mind whether a vegetable grew in the earth or
ripened in the open air. As the beetroot grows deep in the earth,
they are combined with nuts, which grew in light and air. The forces
of earth and light will thus be kept in perfect balance.

4 beautiful round beetroots
2 tablespoonsful margarine
3 tablespoonsful flour
1 teaspoonful chopped fresh coriander
a pinch of sugar
hot water and marmite to taste
200g (7 oz.) chopped nuts or peanuts

Cook the beetroots until they are done, or buy them cooked and
ready from the greengrocer's. After removing the outer skin hollow
them carefully, using a grapefruit knife as this makes the job easier.
Keep the removed pieces as they make an excellent salad for the
next day, combined with some sour apple, a little vinegar and
some oil, and salt and pepper to taste. Make a sauce with the
margarine, the flour and the hot water and marmite. Keep it fairly
thick. Add the chopped nuts (walnuts, hazelnuts, pecans, cashew-
nuts, almonds, etc.,). Even peanuts, though they grow in the earth
as well, so the combination would be less ideal from a biodynamic
view-point, can be useful. Add the chopped coriander greens.

Pour the sauce into the hollowed beetroots, place them in an ovenware dish and heat them thoroughly in a warm oven for fifteen minutes.

Serve them with mashed potatoes and a cucumber salad, or a gherkin. Children will love this meal.

Red Cabbage

There are few things more beautiful and tasty than a gently be-dewed red cabbage on a dreamy autumn morning. The cabbage seems to have absorbed the very spicyness and fragrance of autumn itself. To do the spirit of autumn honour we shall have to eat the red cabbage as it is, uncooked. Should we decide to entrust it to heat, we shall have to be careful. Overcooking red cabbage can change its spicy charm and turn it into a nasty, smelly vegetable.

As a general rule all cabbage should be cooked as shortly as possible. The shorter the time, the better the taste!

We should not have our cabbage cut up in a commercial chopping-machine either.

We buy it whole and cut it up as finely as we wish.

Washing needs to be no more than a token rinse as the tight heart of the cabbage is inaccessible by its very nature to sand and insects.

Red Cabbage Salad

A salad is the simplest way of preparing this wonderful cabbage. Take half a small cabbage, cut it very, very finely and put it in a bowl. Sprinkle a teaspoonful of cumin seeds on the top and pour two cups of boiling water over the cabbage. We take the hardness out of the cabbage without destroying the crispness.

Pour away the water after five minutes and mix into the warm shredded cabbage two tablespoonsful of oil, a tablespoonful of the best herb vinegar, a pinch of sugar and a pinch of salt.

For all its simplicity this is one of the most delicious autumn salads.

Red Cabbage and Celeriac Salad

250g (9 oz.) very finely cut or shredded red cabbage.
½ celeriac root
3 apples

salt, pepper and vinegar or lemon juice to taste
a small carton thick yogurt

Place the finely-shredded red cabbage in a bowl, pour some hot water over it and leave it for fifteen minutes. Strain.

Add the finely-chopped celeriac root and the cubes of apple. Season the salad with salt, pepper and vinegar, or lemon juice. Pour a thin layer of yogurt on top of the salad and mix it at the table, just before serving.

Red Cabbage and Buckwheat

In order to make red cabbage into a more substantial meal, we shall have to cook it, but as quickly as possible, so that we do no damage to the delicate fragrance of autumn.

For four people we shall need:

1 medium-sized red cabbage
300g (11 oz.) whole buckwheat
2 large cooking apples
30g (1¼ oz.) honey

Clean the cabbage, shred it very finely and mix it with the peeled and chopped apples and the whole buckwheat.

Put all the ingredients into a heavy saucepan, add 1 decilitre (3½ fl. oz.) of lukewarm water. Cover and simmer for fifteen minutes.

Serve with honey and lemon juice.

Strange though it may sound: a red cabbage salad tastes well with this dish.

Sauerkraut of Red Cabbage

Remove the outer leaves of a fine, fresh red cabbage. Shred the whole cabbage as finely as possible and add a handful of cumin and dill seeds. Fill an earthenware jar, which may first be rubbed with a clove of garlic, with the mixture.

Use a wooden pestle to beat the cabbage until enough juice has come out to cover the shreds.

Cover the jar with a linen cloth and a wooden lid, weighed down by a stone, so that the cabbage is pressed down properly. Leave the jar in a warm place for one week. After a week the fermenting should have stopped and a cool place is selected for the storing of our red sauerkraut.

It is ready for use after a fortnight and may be used cooked or uncooked.

Sauerkraut with Apples and Raisins.

1000g (2 lb) sauerkraut
a little oil
1 small onion
1 decilitre (3½ fl. oz.) vegetable broth (or white wine)
2 sour apples
sugar or honey

Fry the finely-chopped onion in the oil until golden-brown, and add the washed sauerkraut and the raisins. Finally the vegetable broth or the white wine.

Cook for approximately twenty minutes and add the grated apples. Continue to simmer gently for another fifteen minutes and season with sugar or honey and a little pepper to taste.

Serve the sauerkraut with mashed potatoes or buckwheat purée.

Hotchpotch of Radish Leaves

Buy only radishes whose leaves are still fresh and crisp.

Cut off the leaves, wash them carefully and chop them finely. Mix this in with mashed potatoes just before serving to make it into a filling meal. It is hard to say how many leaves are needed, but normally speaking 1½ kilogrammes (3½ lb) of potatoes are needed for four people to be made into a mash.

At least 500g (1 lb) of freshly-chopped radish leaves should be added. They may be replenished with chopped fresh turnip tops, shredded endive or finely-cut lettuce.

Heat the hotchpotch thoroughly as soon as the leaves have been added and serve immediately.

Radish Salad

Radishes can be eaten as a sandwich filling or sliced onto lettuce, or eaten whole as part of an hors d'oeuvre.

An actual radish-salad is more unusual, but very nice:

3 bunches of radishes
2 tablespoonsful oil
2 tablespoonsful vinegar or lemon juice
salt to taste
2 tablespoonsful thick yogurt
chives

Cut the leaves off the radishes, if fresh keep them for a hotchpotch. Wash the radishes, slice them and sprinkle some salt over them. Leave for fifteen minutes.

Meanwhile make a dressing of the oil, lemon juice or vinegar, a pinch of sugar and the chopped chives. Finally stir in the yogurt and pour this sauce over the radishes, just before serving.

Greens in Sandwiches

There is no better remedy against spring fatigue than a sandwich filled with 'greenery' each day. Make your own mixture of washed and very finely-chopped wild greens like plantain (narrow- or broad-leaved are both allowed), dandelion leaves, garden daisy, ground ivy and yarrow leaves.

In short, whatever you happen to find on a spring walk.

On top of a slice of brown bread with a little butter and marmite, the 'greens' taste good, too.

Soufflé of Garden Cress

A SOUFFLÉ is not a beginner's dish, it belongs to 'Haute Cuisine'. The art of SOUFFLÉ making is in the lightness and airiness of its texture. As soon as it collapses, it is no longer a SOUFFLÉ, but a soggy, revolting disaster.

Some people use a dry cloth to cover the SOUFFLÉ on its journey from the oven to the table.

In short, if you try it, practise a few times before offering this masterpiece to dear friends at an intimate dinner.

2 punnets of garden cress, or a dish of home grown cress
3 large, fresh eggs
1 tablespoonful vegetable oil

2 tablespoonsful wholemeal flour
2-4 dcl (10-14 fl. oz.) warm milk
sea salt, a few drops of garlic juice, if desired

Wash and cut the cress into 2-3cm lengths (or approximately 1 inch). Leave them on a dry cloth, to dry thoroughly.

Make a Hollandaise sauce with the oil, a little garlic juice if desired, the wholemeal flour and the warm milk. Stirring constantly, it should become thick and smooth. Remove from the fire and stir in the dry cress and the loosely-beaten egg yolks. Season the sauce with sea salt or a little marmite. Beat the egg-whites very stiffly in a large bowl and gently fold in the sauce with the cress, using a METAL spoon. Grease a SOUFFLÉ dish, or another ovenware dish, and spoon in the mixture, filling the dish no more than half full. Place the dish in a pre-heated moderate oven (163-177°C/325-350°F/Gas Mark 3-4) and cook it for approximately twenty minutes.

It should double in size and become golden-brown.

Serve straight from the oven with a green salad, if desired.

Garden Cress
The Latin name of garden cress, which is part of the cabbage family, is LEPIDIUM SATIVUM.

This tender green plant, which is related to the radish, is getting more popular every day. Of course, we can buy cress, with or without mustard, from the greengrocer's all year round, but it is more fun to grow your own. It is easy and grows very fast. All you need are:

a packet of garden cress seed
a soup plate
a little potting soil

Fill the plate with the soil and press it down lightly. Evenly spread about one quarter of a packet of seeds. Lightly press the seeds into the earth with the flat of your hand. Spray them with water to 'fasten' them to the earth. Put the plate in a light, warm place and keep it moist.

In about ten days to a fortnight, depending on the temperature,

we can gather our harvest as we only use the sprouts of this plant.
Harvesting is easy, too, just cut through the stems.

Garden Cress in Sandwiches
A slice of brown bread with finely-chopped garden cress and a few drops of lemon juice is healthy and full of vitamins. If desired, a little salt or sugar can be added.

Some chopped-up hard-boiled egg mixed with garden cress make a wonderful sandwich filling.

Green Garden Cress Sauce

1 slice brown bread, without crusts, soaked in milk
1 tablespoonful oil, salt and pepper
1 punnet garden cress
1 bunch of parsley, chopped-up
½ cupful finely-chopped chervil or dill greens
1 pressed clove of garlic

Mix all the ingredients well and serve this sauce with hotchpotch.

Pine Syrup
This is a very old recipe from a country where the pine forests are still large and inpenetrable.

This delightfully fragrant syrup can only be made in May, when the pine trees grow the light-green candles of their new shoots.

Pick a handful of these shoots from the most fragrant pine trees.

Place them upright in well-cleaned jam jars.
Make a syrup of:

500g (1 lb) sugar
1 litre (1¾ pt.) water

Leave it to boil until it has a syrupy consistency and pour it hot over the pine shoots in the jam jars. Cover the jars, but not airtight, and put them, strange though it may sound, in a light place. The old friends who gave me this recipe say that the pine candles need the light to do their job. After a few weeks, somewhere in July, August, the time has come to finish our syrup.

Re-heat the contents of the jars and remove the pine candles with a skimmer. Refill the (clean) jars with the beautifully fragrant syrup, leave them to cool and cover airtight.

Children will love it on bread, but it is also delicious in hot milk or to sweeten any pudding or dessert.

4
Pulses

Pulses are available throughout the year, because they keep so well. That is one of the reasons why they play such an important role in the alternative kitchen. The other, and in fact the main, reason is that they are very rich in vegetable protein. They have an average of about 20 per cent, which is actually higher than average protein content of meat and meat products.

Unfortunately, there is one 'condition' attached to these valuable proteins in pulses. Approximately one third of them have to be eaten in combination with grains, as our bodies can only consume them with the help of the vegetable proteins found in grains and grain products.

At this moment in time it is possible and quite easy to check out this theory by using a complicated chemical formula, but strangely enough, our grandmothers and great-great- grandmothers knew this, although they had never heard of chemistry. They always and automatically served split pea soup with rye bread or gave pancakes afterwards, thus solving the problems of digestion and the absorbing of the proteins. In the modern alternative version we do neither more nor less than our ancestors. We simply follow their example and always serve some sort of grain food when our meal contains a pulse dish, as this will ensure that we receive the full benefit of the vegetable protein in the pulse.

Soy beans (or soya beans) are an exception to this rule: they not only contain far more protein, i.e., approximately 37 per cent, but this protein can be easily and totally absorbed by the body, making it as good if not better than animal protein.

The cook who makes regular use of soya beans, adding a handful here and there, need never be afraid that the family diet will be lacking in protein. However, soya beans, and all other pulses, should be left to soak overnight in plenty of cold water.

Bring them slowly to the boil in the soaking water and simmer gently until the pulse is done.

Adding a small piece of dried seaweed will shorten the cooking time.

Red Kidney Beans and Apple and Onion

250g (9 oz.) red kidney beans
750g (26 oz.) cooking apples
750g (26 oz.) onions
1500g (3½ lb) potatoes
oil, salt

The beans are washed and soaked overnight. The next day the beans are cooked until they are almost done. Meanwhile the onions are chopped finely and fried golden-brown in the oil. Add the peeled and cut-up potatoes and the nearly-cooked beans.

Add a little water if necessary and cook for about thirty minutes, making certain not to overcook this dish, as it will then turn into an unattractive porridge. Meanwhile peel and finely chop the apples and add them just before serving. Heat thoroughly and serve immediately.

A small semolina pudding (remember: pulse and grains!) or a dish of yogurt completes this filling winter meal.

Red Kidney Bean Stew

400g (14 oz.) red kidney beans
2 litres (3½ pt.) water
4 large onions

500g (1 lb) tomatoes
oil, salt, pepper to taste
100g (4 oz.) grated cheese

Wash and soak the beans overnight. Next day bring them to the boil and cook them for approximately one hour or until done. Strain off the excess water (which may be used in soups) and liquidize the beans with a mixer or push them through a sieve. Stir a little milk through the bean PURÉE and pour it into an ovenware dish.

Cover with a layer of golden-brown fried onion rings and peeled, sliced tomatoes. Finally spread the grated cheese on top and brown this delicious bean PURÉE in a warm oven for about twenty minutes.

Serve with a green salad.

A grain and/or milk product should follow this meal in order to ensure correct absorption of the vegetable proteins of the beans.

Red Kidney Beans and Apple

300g (11 oz.) red kidney beans
1½ litres (2¼ pt.) water
1 bay leaf
500g (1 lb) cooking apples
2 tablespoonsful margarine
1 small onion

Soak the beans overnight and cook them with the bay leaf. Strain the beans well, and mix them into the apple sauce, made of the cooking apples and the golden-brown fried onion.

Purée of Green Split Peas

400g (14 oz.) green split peas
2 litres (3½ pt.) water
4 onions
oil, salt

Soak the peas overnight and cook them for 1½ hours, or until soft.
Pass them through a sieve, having strained off the cooking water.

Season with salt and add the onions, finely-chopped and gently stewed in a little oil.

Serve with a salad of fresh vegetables and give a milk product, e.g., yogurt, afterwards.

Green Pea Soup

400g (14 oz.) dried green peas
2 litres (3½ pt.) water
400g (14 oz.) leeks
½ celeriac root
a bunch of celery greens
parsley
salt, pepper and marmite to taste

Soak the beans overnight in the water and cook them for 1½ hours. Strain off the excess water and keep it. Pass the soft peas through a sieve and add the stock again. Chop the celeriac, the leeks and the celery tops finely, add them to the pea soup and simmer gently for at least twenty minutes. Season the soup with salt, pepper and marmite to taste. Serve it with finely-chopped parsley and small pieces of fried bread.

When split peas are used instead of whole dried peas, the vegetables may be cooked with the split peas, instead of being added later on.

French Lentil Soup

1¼ litres (2 pt.) water
250g (9 oz.) lentils
4 small onions
1 clove garlic
3 potatoes
salt, pepper, celery-tops

Soak the lentils overnight in the water and cook them (using the same water), together with the onion-rings and the thinly-sliced clove of garlic. When the lentils are almost done, add the potatoes, cut in small pieces and simmer for thirty minutes more. Pass the soup through a sieve. Add salt and pepper to taste and serve hot, with a sprinkling of finely-chopped celery greens on top.

Sweet and Sour Lentils

400g (14 oz.) lentils
2 litres (3½ pt.) water
1 onion with a clove
2 tablespoonsful margarine
3 tablespoonsful wholemeal flour
1½ cupfuls vegetable broth
1 tablespoonful lemon juice (or wine vinegar)
1 tablespoonful sugar

Soak the lentils overnight and cook them in the water with the onion and the clove. Strain them.

Make a Hollandaise sauce with the margarine, the flour and the vegetable broth. Season it with the lemon juice and the sugar. Add the cooked lentils, heat the sauce thoroughly, add extra lemon juice and/or sugar, if necessary. The taste should be distinctly sweet and sour.

Haricot Beans with Herbs

400g (14 oz.) haricot beans
2 litres (3½ pt.) water
1 bay leaf
3 tablespoonsful oil
2 tablespoonsful chopped chives
1 teaspoonful oregano
1 teaspoonful rosemary
salt to taste

Soak the beans overnight, and cook them with the bay leaf and salt. Strain the beans, but keep them warm in an ovenware dish.

Fry the herbs in the hot oil for a maximum of five minutes.

Spoon the herb sauce over the beans and serve hot. Hard-boiled eggs and a green salad make this into a delicious, well-balanced meal.

Haricot Bean Soup

400g (14 oz.) haricot beans
1½ litres (2¼ pt.) water
4 onions
2 teaspoonsful sweet paprika powder
salt, vinegar or lemon juice
dill or savory to taste

Soak the beans overnight and cook them the next day with the onions, peeled and cut into rings. Pass three-quarters of the beans through a sieve, strain the remainder and add to the soup whole.

Season with the paprika powder, the salt and the fresh (or dried) herbs to taste.

Haricot Bean and Leek Soup

500g (1 lb) haricot beans
1 bay leaf
2 litres (3½ pt.) water
500g (1 lb) leeks
a bunch of celery greens
a bunch of parsley
100g (4 oz.) grated cheese
salt and pepper to taste

Soak the beans overnight and cook them the next morning with the bay leaf for one hour, or until done.

Meanwhile, gently fry the thinly-sliced leeks, the chopped-up celery top and the parsley in a little oil, but take good care not to brown them. Add the leek and herb mixture to the bean soup and simmer gently until the beans are very soft. Add more water if necessary.

Season with salt and pepper and serve this potent soup hot with a sprinkling of grated cheese.

Milanese Minestrone with Haricot Beans

200g (7 oz.) haricot beans or soya beans
1 litre (1¾ pt.) water

2 potatoes
2 tomatoes
2 carrots
a piece of white cabbage
¼ celeriac root
1 onion
1 clove of garlic, if desired
1 cupful of garden peas
2 litres (3½ pt.) boiling water
100g (4 oz.) rice
100g (4 oz.) margarine or oil
100g (4 oz.) grated mature cheese
salt, pepper and sage to taste

Soak the beans overnight and cook them until they are nearly done.

Wash and cut all the vegetables into small pieces and gently fry them in the margarine (or oil) without browning them. Add the boiling water and simmer for ten minutes, until all the vegetables are done. Add the salt, the pepper and the rice and simmer for another fifteen minutes.

Stir in the grated cheese just before serving, or serve it separately so everyone can help themselves.

French bread or toast are served with this soup.

5

Mushrooms

In autumn nature surprises us with her most mysterious crop. One day there is nothing, the next day there are mushrooms in the woods.

Now that nature is in danger, it is best to leave all mushrooms and toadstools alone. To pick the inedible ones is indubitably a waste of this mysterious growth.

Should we give in to the temptation of picking a few golden coloured chanterelles or a single rust-brown boletus, we should only pick a single one of a group.

Therefore the recipes given in this chapter are about wild mushrooms, but they can easily be substituted by cultural ones from the shop. The shop mushrooms are much less fragrant than real mushrooms from the woods, however.

It is even possible now to grow one's own mushrooms, in which case we can at least be certain that they will be fresh, free from pesticides and the result of our own loving care.

All mushrooms, the real wild ones and the cultured ones, should be washed, cleaned and used as soon as we bring them home, for mushrooms are fresh and crisp for a day only. They wilt as quickly as they come up so we have to make use of the unique opportunity as it presents itself to us.

Fried Mushrooms

The simplest way of preparing mushrooms is frying them quickly in a little margarine or oil. They can be eaten on toast, in an omelette or with potatoes, rice or millet.

We need:

250g (9 oz.) cleaned, thinly sliced mushrooms
2 tablespoonsful sunflower oil
1 onion
a little sea salt
1 tablespoonful finely chopped parsley

First we fry the onion, finely chopped, until it is golden-brown. Then we add the mushrooms and fry them quickly, moving the frying pan back and forth for a few minutes. Do not let them simmer, as this will turn the beautiful fragrant fruit of the woods into tasteless, leathery bits of nothing. Add the salt and the chopped parsley and heat thoroughly. Serve immediately.

Potatoes Stuffed with Mushrooms

For four people we need:

8 large potatoes
3 cupsful cooked millet, rice or potato
4 tablespoonsful grated cheese
200g (7 oz.) mushrooms
1 small onion
1 tablespoonful finely chopped parsley
2 tablespoonsful sunflower oil

Scrub the potatoes clean and cook them, unpeeled, in water. Simmer them gently so that the skin remains unbroken. When they are done, leave them to cool off a little. Peel the potatoes, cut them in half and scoop each half out carefully.

Arrange the hollow halves nicely on an oiled baking tray or in a large ovenware dish. Fill them with a mixture of mushrooms, that have been quickly fried with the onion, millet, rice or potato, the chopped-up parsley, the grated cheese and a little tamari for taste if desired.

Add a little more sunflower oil to the baking tray and bake the potatoes in about twenty minutes or until golden-brown and piping hot.

This recipe can be made without an oven in a large heavy saucepan. The potatoes are simply heated thoroughly over a very low fire. We shall have to do without the golden crust.

This will make a good meal for four people, which can be supplemented with a salad, if desired.

Chanterelles in Batter

250g (9 oz.) chanterelles
1 egg
milk, flour
oil for frying

Wash the chanterelles carefully and thoroughly, and leave them to drain well, preferably on a piece of kitchen paper.

Make a pancake batter of the egg with some milk and flour.

Dip the chanterelles into the batter and deep fry them quickly until they are golden-brown. Serve them immediately, seasoned with a little sea salt. They go well with mashed potatoes or boiled rice.

Stewed Cep

The ceps are very tasty as long as they are white and spongy inside. When picking them, this should be checked.

This delicious autumny dish requires:

450g (1 lb) onions
300g (11 oz.) ceps
oil
salt and pepper to taste

Gently fry the finely-chopped onions in the oil, but do not brown them. Add the sliced ceps and gently simmer for five minutes. Season with salt and pepper and serve hot with rice, buckwheat or on toast.

Mushroom Salad

250g (9 oz.) mushrooms
lemon juice
oil
salt, pepper to taste
chopped parsley

Wash the mushrooms and slice them thinly. Pour on some fresh lemon juice to avoid discolouring.

Season with salt, pepper and chopped parsley to taste and add a few drops of oil.

Toss and serve immediately.

Mushrooms and Nuts
Button mushrooms are a common article in the shops today. Provided they are prepared well, they are delicious with rice or mashed potatoes.
We need:

250g (9 oz.) button mushrooms
1 tablespoonful vegetable oil
100g (4 oz.) cashews (or other nuts)
100g (4 oz.) raisins
1 tin of tomato PURÉE
flour
marmite for seasoning

Wash the mushrooms. Leave the small ones whole, slice the larger ones, fry them quickly in the oil, add the chopped nuts and the raisins that have soaked in water for twenty-four hours.

Mix in a bowl the tomato PURÉE with a tablespoonful of flour, a teaspoonful of marmite and 1½ cupsful of hot water.

Pour the mixture into the saucepan with the mushrooms and the nuts. Simmer for a minute or until hot, but do not overcook. Serve hot with boiled rice and a salad.

Mushrooms in Sour Cream Sauce

500g (1 lb) mushrooms
lemon juice
1 cupful vegetable broth
2 tablespoonsful margarine
3 tablespoonsful flour
1 dcl (3¼ fl. oz.) sour cream
2 cupsful of mushroom broth
1 tablespoonful finely chopped parsley

Clean the mushrooms, wash them and put them in water with lemon juice to avoid discolouring.

Slice them once lengthwise and cook them for maximum five minutes in the broth. Lift them out of the broth and leave them to drain.

Make a Hollandaise sauce of the margarine, the flour, the sour cream and the broth. Do not make it too thick. Add the cooked mushrooms and sprinkle the parsley over the top. Serve piping hot with potatoes, rice or noodles.

6
Potatoes

The potato, whose Latin name is SOLANUM TUBEROSUM, is a member of the SOLANACEAE, or Nightshade family, a family which counts quite a few poisonous plants among its members, such as the ATROPA BELLA DONNA or Deadly Nightshade, which produces the deadly poisonous Bella Donna, and the NICOTIANA or Tobacco plant, which gives us its anything-but-harmless leaves.

On the other hand, the tomato and the Spanish and the Sweet Pepper are members of this illustrious family as well, which should restore some of its good name. The potato itself is a borderline case: its tubers, which we eat under the name of potato, are indeed edible, but they are the only part of the plant that are. All other parts are poisonous. This fact has not made the introduction of the potato from America into Western Europe easy.

It was in the beginning of the seventeenth century that the first potatoes arrived at the French Court from America. A few months later a banquet was prepared for the Court, using the small green fruits of the potato plant. All participants became violently ill, and the king was so angry that he ordered all potato plants torn out and burned. This was done, of course, but a hungry gardener's apprentice could not resist the smell, took his chance and ate the tubers. They were tasty and the boy did not become ill. This news reached the king's ears and it confirmed the messages which he had recieved from America in the meanwhile.

However, the king decided that he had had enough after one disastrous dinner and he would have no more of the potato, which was grown as a curio in a sheltered corner of the palace garden. This proved to be a very lucky foresight more than one and a half centuries later.

Hunger reigned in 1769 and held western Europe in its iron grip, because the grain harvests had failed. Monsieur Parmentier, a minister under King Louis XV, was willing to give the ill-favoured potato another chance. With the king's permission he used a trick in order to remove the suspicion against the foreign crop. He had a well-ploughed, well-fenced field planted with potatoes and he had notices stuck to the fence with the words: 'It is strictly prohibited to take these tubers, as they are intended for the king's table.'

The notices did their job. Before they were even fully grown, every single potato was stolen and eaten by the poor farmers.

The cleverest farmers kept a few and planted them in their gardens Thus the potato - mockingly called 'royal tuber' for a while - began its triumphant victory of western Europe, replacing part of the grains in the daily diet as its popularity increased.

Nowadays the potato is very much part of our staple diet. It has earned its place in our kitchen, for this cheap plant forms one of our most important sources of vitamin C and vegetable proteins, provided the potatoes are peeled thinly. The potato, like the grains, also has a very high carbohydrate content.

If the potato is not used as part of a dish, it is best to cook it in the well-scrubbed skin. Peel just before serving, or let each member of the family peel their own at the table. It is soon learned and this way of cooking preserves the precious vitamins and proteins, which are stored directly under the skin.

Potato Goulash

When the Hungarian farmer's wife has meat in the house, she will make a meat goulash, but when she hasn't she will make her goulash with potatoes, which tastes just as well.
We will need:

750g (1½ lb) potatoes

500g (1 lb) onions
3 tablespoonsful vegetable oil
3 teaspoonsful sweet paprika powder
a little broth
a dash of cream

Peel and chop the onions finely and fry them in the oil, letting them get soft and very light-brown. Add the paprika powder and finally the potatoes, cut in small cubes the size of small new potatoes.

If the cubes are too small the gulash may become mushy, if they are too big it will take too long.

Fry the potato cubes with the onions and paprika powder for a few minutes and add the broth or hot water and marmite.

Cover the saucepan and simmer slowly over very low heat for approximately twenty minutes. Give the saucepan a little shake now and then to avoid burning.

Add a little cream just before serving and serve this goulash as hot as possible.

A green salad goes well with it.

Potato Croquettes

400g (14 oz.) mashed potato
1 tablespoonful finely chopped onion
1 tablespoonful flour
100g (4 oz.) chopped mixed nuts
1 egg
breadcrumbs
oil for frying

Mix the mashed potatoes with the finely-chopped onion, the flour and the chopped nuts into a thick dough-like mass. Form little croquettes, or flat round pancakes, roll them through the loosely-beaten egg and through the breadcrumbs.

Fry in oil until they are golden-brown. Serve with a green salad.

Potato Omelette

500g (1 lb) boiled potatoes
200g (7 oz.) onions
3 eggs
salt, pepper and fresh herbs for seasoning
oil for frying

Slice the boiled potatoes, fry the chopped onions gently in a little oil until they are soft. Add them to the potatoes. Season the potato and onion mixture with salt, pepper and fresh green herbs, such as chives, parsley, celery tops, finely chopped. Loosely beat the eggs and pour them over the potatoes.

Fry in a heavy frying pan. The result will be a thick, fragrant and beautiful omelette.

Hotchpotch
For the benefit of all those people who do not know how to make a traditional hotchpotch, a recipe has been included.

There will be enough for four hungry eaters.

200g (4½ lb) potatoes
water, salt
2 dcl (7 fl. oz.) milk
100g (4 oz.) vegetable margarine
600g (21oz.) young, fresh and finely chopped vegetables

Peel the potatoes and boil them till they are done. Strain, steam them dry and mash them with the margarine (or a cupful of vegetable oil) and the milk. Season the mash with salt, pepper and spices, such as nutmeg, or fresh herbs and then add the washed vegetables. Heat the hotchpotch thoroughly, stirring all the time and serve immediately.

A cheese sauce, a vegetable or nut-sauce taste well with this basic hotchpotch. A slice of cheese (Gouda or Edam) dipped in a flour, water and salt batter, rolled in breadcrumbs and fried golden-brown makes a good combination, too.

Hotchpotch and Cheese
Make a basic hotchpotch as described above and add small cubes of mild cheese at the last moment.

Approximately 50g (2 oz.) per person. Heat the hotchpotch thoroughly, but make sure that the cheese does not melt.

It stands to reason that, apart from the traditional vegetables used in a hotchpotch, such as spinach, young endive or turnip tops, the spicy, fragrant greens from the field can also be used in this dish. Provided everything is washed well and chopped very finely.

Potato Salad

1kg (3¼ lb) potatoes
2 tablespoonsful oil
3 tablespoonsful flour
a cupful of milk
salt, pepper, cumin seed, sweet basil
1 egg yolk
the juice of 1 lemon
1 onion, dill and parsley

Scrub the potatoes clean and cook them in plenty of water. Make certain that the potatoes are of the kind that do not go mushy. Peel them, while they are still warm, and slice them. Arrange them in a bowl.

Make a sauce of the oil, the flour and the warm milk.

Season the sauce with cumin seeds, sweet basil, salt and pepper. Remove from the heat, stir in the egg yolk and the finely-chopped onion, and finally the lemon juice. Pour the hot sauce over the sliced potatoes. Chill the salad thoroughly and garnish it with finely chopped dill and parsley just before serving.

Serve it with baked cauliflower, or salsify.

Potato and Leek Soup
This autumny soup is a marvellous one to feed to chilly, hungry people. It is satisfying enough to be served as a main course.

Very large eaters may want a small bowl of muesli or a buckwheat pancake to round off the meal, but ordinarily this should not be necessary. An apple is really all a normal eater will want after this

filling soup.
  You will need:

1kg (2¼ lb) leeks
2 onions
50g (2 oz.) sunflower oil
1¼ litres (2 pt.) water
750g (1¾ lb) potatoes
3 cupsful milk
salt, pepper, marjoram
1/8 litre (¼ pt.) cream
½ cupful finely-chopped green sweet pepper.

Use only the white parts of the leeks, wash them very well and cut them into 1cm (1¼ inch) thick slices.
  Chop the onions finely and fry them gently in the oil until they are soft.
  Add the sliced leeks, heat thoroughly before adding the water. Cover, bring to the boil and simmer for approximately ten minutes. Add the peeled potatoes, cut into small cubes, add a little more water if necessary and simmer for another ten minutes. When the potatoes are nearly done, add the milk and the herbs and simmer for ten more minutes. Take care not to let the potatoes become mushy and overcooked.
  Just before serving the cream is added and at the very last moment we sprinkle the chopped pepper on top.
  Some people like to eat a slice of brown bread with this soup, and why not?

Polish Potatoes

8 large potatoes
100g (4 oz.) mushrooms
150g (5 oz.) grated cheese
2 tablespoonsful margarine
3 tablespoonsful flour
1 cupful milk
parsley and rosemary

Peel the potatoes and boil them in water until they are half cooked. Using a grapefruit knife, scoop out as much of the potatoes as possible. Slice a little bit off each hollowed-out potato so that they can be placed upright in a buttered ovenware dish.

Chop up the scooped-out potato and mix it with the quickly-fried, sliced mushrooms, half the grated cheese, a little salt, pepper, the rosemary and a generous amount of chopped-up parsley.

Fill the scooped-out potatoes with the potato and mushroom mixture.

Make a Hollandaise sauce with the margarine, the flour and the milk - adding a little broth if necessary. Stir in the remainder of the cheese and pour the sauce over the stuffed potatoes. Place the dish in a moderately hot oven and bake the potatoes for approximately twenty minutes, or until they are piping hot and golden-brown.

This sounds like a complicated dish, but after one has done it a couple of times, it is really quite easy and most people will love it.

Potato and Onion Dish
Another favourite for hungry eaters on a chilly day.
The ingredients are:

750g (1¾ lb) potatoes
500g (1 lb) small onions
a little lemon juice
1 tablespoonful flour
1 cupful vegetable broth
salt, pepper, a knob of butter
marjoram for seasoning

Peel the onions, leave them whole and simmer them in a little water and lemon juice till they are done.

Put a layer of potato slices in a buttered ovenware dish, cover them with a layer of drained cooked onions, topped by potatoes again, and so on until all the onions and sliced potatoes have been used.

Mix the flour, salt, pepper and marjoram into the vegetable broth and pour the mixture over the layers of vegetables.

Place the dish in a warm oven and cook it for 30-35 minutes, or until done and golden-brown.

Tomato Chutney

A delicious chutney made of tomatoes, especially for people who love hot, spicy things.

500g (1 lb) tomatoes
3 cloves garlic
1 small onion
1 fresh red Spanish pepper
2 teaspoonsful ginger powder

Remove the stem and the seeds of the red pepper and cut it up very finely. Cut a cross over the top of the tomatoes, pour boiling hot water over them, peel them and cut them in quarters. Remove all seeds and mushy bits, leaving only the hard flesh of the tomatoes.

Put the tomatoes, the juice of two cloves of garlic, the chopped pepper, the finely-chopped onion, salt to taste, the ginger powder and two tablespoonsful of water in a saucepan and simmer for just over thirty minutes.

Add a little more water if it should boil down too much and become too dry.

Leave it to cool and pour the chutney into well-cleaned jam jars and keep them in a cool place.

This chutney is strictly for adults and will keep for several weeks.

7

Buckwheat

To mention buckwheat in one breath with the other grains is a common mistake. Buckwheat is not a 'wheat' at all, in fact it is not even remotely related to the large family of assorted grasses.

Buckwheat is actually a member of the POLYGONACEA family, to which rhubarb and sorrel belong as well.

Whereas the two latter ones are used as a vegetable, buckwheat, whose official Latin name is FAGOPYRUM SAGITTATUM, is grown exclusively for its seeds. The seeds are hard and triangular in shape and look very similar to beach-nuts.

Buckwheat is an annual plant, native to our soil and a very remarkable plant at that.

Buckwheat will not grow on chemically fertilized soil. Moreover, it is so strong and healthy that no known disease or pest can harm it. Therefore we can be sure that we have a crop which is purely natural, i.e., has never been sprayed with insecticides or been grown on artificially fertilized land. And that is more than we can say with certainty of almost every other agricultural or horticultural product. In earlier days buckwheat used to be an important food, especially in the poor, sandy regions, as buckwheat is one of the few 'grains' which do exceptionally well on poor, sandy soil. The seeds were cracked, the outer skin removed and the kernels were broken up and sold under the name of buckwheat groats and made into a thick porridge. When the kernels were finely ground, it made buckwheat flour, and until a few decades ago this flour was an indispensable ingredient of pancakes, drop scones and the like.

Mixed with other flours, it could also be used for bread-making.

During the last few decades buckwheat has lost its popularity, together with many other healthy and simple, old-fashioned foods. However, it is still being grown today, mainly because the kernel contains the healing agent 'Rutin', which is used among others in the struggle against arteriosclerosis, i.e., the hardening of the arteries.

Isn't it strange that it seems to occur to very few people, that it would be much healthier, easier and a lot cheaper to eat a little more buckwheat, instead of swallowing expensive pills containing 'Rutin'.

It stands to reason that we have included a number of buckwheat recipes in this alternative cookbook, not in the least because of its richness in protective ingredients.

Buckwheat Porridge
This delicious and nourishing porridge can be eaten hot for breakfast, or it can be left to cool and stiffen, so that we can make it into lovely buckwheat pancakes for supper.

For the porridge is needed:

1¼ litres (2 pt.) milk
250g (9 oz.) whole buckwheat
honey or golden syrup

Bring the milk to the boil, add the buckwheat and simmer for at least fifteen minutes, or until the buckwheat is done, over a very low heat. Serve hot with honey or golden syrup.

Leave the remainder to cool and stiffen, to be used the next day or in the evening, making:

Buckwheat Pancakes
Cut the stiff, cold porridge into slices, dip them in egg and in flour and fry them golden-brown in a little hot sunflower-oil.

Serve them with brown sugar as a dessert after soup or a light salad.

Buckwheat and Cheese Dish

Make a buckwheat porridge as described above.

Mix 3 egg yolks, 150g (5 oz.) grated, mature cheese and a little sea salt and add this to the porridge. Beat the eggwhites very stiffly and fold them into the buckwheat, egg and cheese mixture.

Pour it into a buttered ovenware dish and bake it golden-brown for approximately thirty minutes in a moderate oven. It can also be done in a frying pan, covered and turned over once after about fifteen minutes. Use a very, very low heat.

Sprinkle a handful of finely-chopped parsley over the buckwheat-'SOUFFLÉ', just before serving.

Serve it with a crisp green salad of vegetables (wild or cultivated) of the season and it will be a healthy and satisfying meal.

Buckwheat Risotto

For 4 large eaters you will need:

1 litre (1¾ pt.) boiling water
500g (1 lb) whole buckwheat
1 large onion
3 tablespoonsful sunflower-oil
100g (4 oz.) finely-chopped carrots
100g (4 oz.) garden peas
parsley
sea salt

Gently fry the very finely-chopped onion and the buckwheat kernels until they are soft and very light brown.

Pour exactly 1 litre (1¾ pt.) boiling water over the onion and buckwheat, add the vegetables, cover and simmer for twenty minutes over very low heat. Garnish with the finely chopped, fresh parsley and serve this 'risotto' with a spicy peanut sauce.

Buckwheat and Tomato

500g (1 lb) buckwheat
1 large onion
3 tablespoonsful sunflower-oil
250g (9 oz.) peeled and chopped tomatoes

**1 tablespoonful finely chopped green sweet pepper
parsley and sea salt for seasoning**

Gently fry the onion and the buckwheat until soft and very light
brown, add the green pepper, the tomatoes and a little water with
some salt (or marmite). Simmer for twenty minutes until the
buckwheat is done.
 Serve this dish with a cheese sauce and/or a crisp, green salad.

Buckwheat Croquettes

Should we feel like giving the family a treat, Buckwheat Croquettes
served with a tomato or a cucumber salad (or both), make a
delicious meal.
 For four people you will need:

**200g (7 oz.) whole buckwheat
2 tablespoonsful sunflower-oil
1 large onion
1 teaspoonful coriander
2 tablespoonsful buckwheat (or wholemeal) flour
2 eggs
breadcrumbs
salt for seasoning
dill, parsley or chives if desired**

Measure the buckwheat, add twice the quantity of water and cook
it for about twenty minutes.
 Meanwhile fry the very finely-chopped onion and the coriander
golden-brown. Loosely beat the eggs, add the flour and pour the
mixture onto the onions stirring all the time. Add some chopped-up
green herbs if desired, like dill, chives or parsley. Mix all ingredients
with the cooked buckwheat and roll the mixture into small
croquettes. Cover the croquettes with breadcrumbs and fry them in
ample hot sunflower oil until crisp and golden-brown. Serve them
immediately and piping hot.

Buckwheat Purée

250g (9 oz.) whole buckwheat

2 tablespoonsful sunflower-oil
finely-chopped celery tops and parsley
1 litre (1¾ pt.) water
sea salt

Fry the buckwheat until it is light-brown in the hot oil, add the water and salt to taste and cook it in about twenty minutes.

Pass the cooked buckwheat kernels through a sieve, but add the silvery skins to the PURÉE again, should any be left behind in the sieve.

Stir in the chopped green herbs, heat the PURÉE thoroughly and serve it with beetroots or red cabbage, or any other cabbage.

Buckwheat with Cabbage and Cheese

4 cupsful buckwheat
6 cupsful water
sea salt
a little tamari (i.e., sesame oil)
200g (7 oz.) sliced cheese
white cabbage leaves
oil

Toast the buckwheat kernels in a dry saucepan. Add six cups (1½ times the quantity of the buckwheat) of water and a little sea salt to taste and cook it in fifteen minutes over a low heat. Add a dash of tamari.

Stew the cabbage leaves in a little oil, but do not overcook. They should remain crisp.

Arrange a few cabbage leaves on a pre-heated dish, add a little sliced cheese, some cabbage leaves again, a little more cheese and finally the cooked buckwheat.

Serve as hot as possible.

Buckwheat à la Anne Marie

4 cupsful buckwheat
6 cupsful water
sea salt

2 tablespoonsful vegetable oil
4 tablespoonsful wholemeal flour
3 onions
2 cupsful finely chopped vegetables of the season
(including mushrooms)

Toast the buckwheat and cook it with the water and salt. Meanwhile make a Hollandaise sauce of the oil and the flour and some water, stirring all the time. Stew the finely-chopped onions and the vegetables in a little oil and add them to the sauce. Bring to the boil and simmer for a minute.

Put the cooked buckwheat into a buttered ovenware dish, add the vegetable sauce and cook this dish for half an hour in a moderate oven till it is piping hot and beautifully fragrant.

8
Millet

Millet or PANICUM MILIACEUM belongs to the large family of grasses, as do most other grains.

It has dry kernel-like seeds, which are easily stored and keep well. Millet, like most other grains, is rich in carbohydrates, proteins and vitamins and it makes a satisfactory, though not perfect, main food source if eaten alone without any additional foods.

Comparatively speaking, millet has a higher protein content than most other grains, which makes it very valuable in the alternative kitchen with its vegetarian character.

Unfortunately millet is little known in this country and therefore little used or loved. One can search for recipes on millet in old cookery books and find none at all. This is understandable as millet does not grow well in our climate. It needs long warm summers for its proper development.

In central and southern Europe millet is well known, especially in the national, traditional kitchen. Unfortunately, the Welfare State has wiped many a healthy and simple food off the table. In spite of this, we still find the occasional millet dish appearing on the tables of central and southern Europe, ·mainly because millet is easy and quick to prepare. The actual cooking-time of millet is between seven and ten minutes.

One can use the small, yellow kernels in all those recipes that are ordinarily made with rice, full wheat kernels, groats or other grains. Millet can be used as a substitute for all and any of those grains.

It combines well with herbs and vegetables; in sauces and soups it can be used as a binder and it can successfully be cooked into a porridge.

The advantage of millet over other kinds of grains is the short cooking time. The fact that many people will have to get used to the taste could be mentioned as a disadvantage.

Dry Cooked Millet

4 cupsful millet
8 cupsful water
sea salt for seasoning

Bring the millet, the water and the salt to the boil, cover the saucepan and cook it over a very low fire in 10 to 15 minutes, or until dry and done.

Savoury Millet Cakes

3 cupsful millet
4 cupsful water
sea salt to taste
1 tablespoonful vegetable margarine
1 tablespoonful wholemeal flour
2 fresh eggs

Cook the millet in the water with a little sea salt. The porridge will thicken very quickly as relatively little water is being used. Remove the saucepan from the fire, stir in the margarine, the flour and the loosely-beaten eggs. Season, adding pepper and chopped green herbs, if desired. Make the mixture into nice round cakes and bake them golden-brown in a warm oven for approximately fifteen minutes. Serve the savoury millet cakes hot with cooked pulse and/or stewed vegetables.

Couscous of Millet with Fried Cheese

4 cupsful millet
8 cupsful water
4 small onions
oil
sea salt to taste

Toast the millet kernels golden-brown and add the water. Bring it to the boil and cook it for ten to fifteen minutes, or until dry and done.

Meanwhile, fry the finely-chopped onion in a little oil, until it is golden coloured and serve it with the couscous, seasoned to taste with sea salt. Fried Cheese Slices (see p. 120) and stewed fresh vegetables taste good with this dish.

Puréed Millet

4 cupsful millet
8 cupsful water
sea salt to taste
1 tablespoonful sunflower-oil
1 large onion
parsley

Cook the millet in the usual way. Pass it through a sieve while still hot, season with a little sea salt and heat again.

Meanwhile, gently fry the finely-chopped onion in the hot oil, add the chopped fresh parsley at the last moment and pour this mixture over the millet PURÉE in the serving dish. Millet PURÉE is very similar in taste to mashed potatoes, but is far more nutritious.

The given quantity of millet PURÉE, served with a large helping of green salad with some sesame seed or sunflower kernels, makes a totally adequate main meal, without the need for a starter or a dessert.

Millet Pudding

2 cupsful millet

5 to 6 cupsful milk with water
sugar or honey for sweetening

Stir the millet into the boiling milk and water and gently simmer it over very low heat for thirty minutes, or until the millet is very well done. Remove from the fire and whisk thoroughly - or use a mixer - to make the porridge very smooth. Sweeten it with honey or brown sugar and pour it into a pudding-dish.

Leave to cool.

Serve cold, with preserved or fresh fruit or garnish the millet pudding with crystalized rose petals.

Millet Risotto

A name, which is actually wrong, as risotto means rice dish, but all grain and vegetable dishes prepared like a risotto are nowadays known under that name.

4 cupsful millet
8 cupsful water
2 onions
2 cupsful finely chopped cauliflower and celery
2 tablespoonsful sunflower oil
grated cheese

Cook the millet according to the basic recipe.

Meanwhile, fry the onions and the finely-chopped vegetables in the oil. Add the cooked millet and mix thoroughly.

Serve piping hot with a generous helping of grated cheese, in order to heighten the protein level of this dish.

Millet and Potato Dish

500g (1 lb) potatoes, milk, salt
2 cupsful millet
4 cupsful water
100g (4 oz.) grated cheese
1 onion
100g (4 oz.) mushrooms
green herbs and sea salt to taste

Mash the potatoes with the milk and season them. Butter a large ovenware dish and fill it with the mashed potatoes.

Cook the millet in the ordinary way, while the chopped onion and mushrooms fry gently in a little oil. Add the millet to the onion and mushroom mixture, as well as the grated cheese and mix thoroughly. Season with a little sea salt and add the mixture to the potatoes in the ovenware dish.

Sprinkle a little more cheese on the top and cook it in a warm oven for approximately twenty minutes.

When it is hot and golden-brown, serve immediately.

Muesli of Millet Flakes

For this recipe the millet flakes should preferably be toasted, as this will enhance the taste of the muesli.

8 tablespoonsful toasted millet flakes
3 tablespoonsful raisins
3 apples
½ cupful finely-chopped nuts
juice of 1 lemon
1 glass of milk or yogurt
honey or brown sugar

Soak the raisins in a little water overnight. Carefully strain off the water and mix the raisins the next morning with the freshly-toasted millet flakes, the grated apples, the lemon juice and the chopped nuts. Add the milk or yogurt just before serving and sweeten the muesli with honey or brown sugar. Divide over four bowls and serve as a breakfast cereal or a light dessert.

9

Groats or Barley

The very fact that one plant is known under two totally different names proves its popularity. Groats and barley are one and the same thing, i.e., the seed kernels of the barley plant or HORDEUM, which is a member of the grass/grains family.

The name groats is ordinarily used for the kernel in the husk, whereas barley usually means the hulled variety.

The plant barley feels wonderfully at home in the Low Countries near the sea and one can even find many different kinds of wild barley there. The best known species are Mouse barley, or HORDEUM MURINUM, and Sea barley, which prefers silt for its habitat and thrives on the islands and sea-dikes and has the Latin name of HORDEUM MARINUM.

The ancient Germanic tribes knew how to put barley to good use. The oldest known barley recipe comes from them in the form of barley broth, a strong ale brewed with barley.

Apart from beer brewing, barley was used and still is used in bread making, in pancake batter and many other doughy foods.

With the older generation barley will still be known for its binding qualities when preparing soups or puddings.

Barley truly deserves a place in our daily diet as it is - like millet - high in proteins. Its average protein content is round about 10 per cent. A disadvantage of groats/barley is the long cooking time. The kernels need to cook for a minimum time of forty-five minutes before they are soft and done. On the other hand, barley dishes are very tasty and usually a great success with children.

Almost every recipe that uses a whole grain kind, can also be made with barley. It deserves recommendation, however, to give all barley dishes a nice crisp and brown crust in the oven before serving. This crust should not be looked upon as a mere luxury. It serves a definite purpose, as the smooth and gelatinous kernels of barley are so easily swallowed with chewing. The crust makes chewing necessary, and chewing well is an essential part of good and healthy eating.

Before going into the recipe section of this chapter, we would like to include an old tip to young nursing mothers: Barley-water, made by simmering a little barley in a lot of water for several hours, is a cheap and effective method of ensuring a steady supply of milk for the baby.

Dry Cooked Barley

300g (11 oz.) barley
1 litre (1¾ pt.) water
a little salt

Wash the barley and soak it in 1 litre (1¾ pt.) of water (definitely no more) overnight. Bring the barley and water to the boil stirring constantly, add a little sea salt and cover it well. Leave it to simmer over a very low heat. Dry cooked barley can be used like dry cooked rice and tastes delicious with all kinds of vegetables and fruits.

Barley and Mushrooms

300g (11 oz.) barley
1 litre (1¾ pt.) vegetable broth
sunflower oil
2 onions
200g (7 oz.) mushrooms
salt to taste
dill or thyme

Toast the barley in a little oil in a heavy saucepan and stir in the vegetable broth.

Meanwhile gently fry the chopped onions, until they are soft and add them to the barley.

Leave to simmer over very low heat for one hour, or until dry and done.

Fry the mushrooms quickly and mix them with the cooked barley just before serving.

Season to taste with a little sea salt and some dill or thyme if desired.

Barley and Lentil Dish
A delicious and filling meal that can be prepared in a very short time, provided the barley and lentils are ready and cooked beforehand. No oven is needed. It is served hot with a mixed green salad.

150g (5 oz.) soaked and cooked lentils
150g (5 oz.) soaked and cooked barley
3 onions
100g (4 oz.) mushrooms
75g (3 oz.) sunflower oil
75g (3 oz.) peeled sunflower kernels

Fry the chopped onions over a very gentle heat, add the sunflower kernels and finally, when the onions are soft and light-brown, the mushrooms. The lentils and barley are added when everything is thoroughly hot and fragrant. Heat for a few more minutes and serve piping hot with a generous helping of freshly picked and chopped parsley and chives. A large mixed or green salad is the perfect companion to this dish.

Barley and Prunes
This delicious old-fashioned pudding used to be called 'water-gruel'. Preferably serve it after a light main course, but not after a salad, as it is slightly acid in character.

100g (4 oz.) pearl-barley
250g (9 oz.) prunes
water

a slice of lemon peel
lemon juice
blackcurrant juice
sugar or honey

Leave the barley and the prunes to soak overnight in separate bowls. Cook them the next day and mix them when both are done. Add a slice of lemon peel, the juice of a lemon and a dash of blackberry juice if desired.

Bring this refreshing dessert to taste with brown sugar or honey. It can be eaten immediately or left to cool and eaten cold.

Preferably serve this dish after a main dish including pulse, as the proteins of the barley aid the body to fully absorb the proteins of the pulse.

Barley and Nut Dish

300g (11 oz.) barley
1 litre (1¾ pt.) water
2 large onions
200g (7 oz.) chopped nuts or 200g (7 oz.) peanut butter
2 eggs
2 tablespoonsful oil
2 tablespoonsful flour
1/8 litre (¼ pt.) vegetable broth

Soak the barley overnight in the litre of water. Bring to the boil the next morning stirring constantly. Cook for one hour over very low heat. Meanwhile cook a sauce.

Fry the chopped onions gently in a little sunflower oil, add the flour and gradually add the broth, stirring vigorously all the time.

Remove the saucepan from the heat and whisk in the eggs. Add the nuts or the peanut butter, mixed with a tablespoonful of water if it is too thick. Stir the sauce into the cooked barley and put the mixture into a buttered ovenware dish.

Bake in the oven until it has a lovely brown crust and serve it with boiled cauliflower or any other fresh vegetable.

Barley and Raisins

150g (5 oz.) barley
100g (4 oz.) raisins
6dcl (21 fl. oz.) water

Wash the barley and the raisins and soak them together overnight in water. Bring them to the boil the next day, stirring constantly and cook them for one hour over a very low heat.

When the barley is dry and cooked serve it with molten honey as a dessert after a soup, or as an entrée before a meal of vegetables.

10
Oats

Oats (AVENA SATIVA) are known to be good for horses. As the number of horses in this country diminishes every year, a smaller quantity of oats is grown these days.

This is a great pity, as we are just rediscovering the value of oats. Oats are not only very good for horses, they are also very good for people too. We, however, do not eat the whole kernel, which is too hard to digest, but we eat oak flakes or porridge oats.

Both products are made from the whole kernel, which is first peeled and then steamed.

Porridge oats are flattened as well. We even distinguish between ordinary porridge oats and fast cooking oats, the only difference being the fact that the latter has been steamed longer, so takes less time to cook.

Oats are real champions among the wheats for two reasons: firstly, the protein content of oat flakes is 13 to 15 per cent, which is considerably higher than that of other grains; secondly, oats are rich in polyunsaturated fats. As most people will realize, polyunsaturated fats are of great importance to us as they lower the cholesterol level of the blood.

To put it in simple terms: a diet that is rich in oats can help prevent arteriosclerosis (or hardening of the arteries).

Apart from these two prominent good qualities oats are also rich in trace minerals and vitamins, e.g., vitamin B1.

In short, a healthy and versatile food product that should be included on our daily menu, if only in the form of muesli - or porridge.

Oatcakes with Paprika

100g (4 oz.) oats
2 tablespoonsful wholemeal flour
1 onion
1 egg
2 tablespoonsful vegetable broth
2 tablespoonsful milk
2 teaspoonsful paprika powder
salt and pepper to taste
breadcrumbs
oil for frying

Mix the oats, the flour, the loosely-beaten egg, the finely-chopped and gently-fried onion, the vegetable stock, the milk and the paprika powder together and make into a dough-like paste. Season with salt and pepper. Form four flat round cakes, coat them with the breadcrumbs and fry them in a little oil for approximately ten minutes, or until the oat cakes are golden-brown and done.

Serve them with steamed vegetables to make a complete meal, or serve them as a hot snack with a sandwich lunch or at teatime.

Oatcakes with Cheese

100g (4 oz.) oats
2 tablespoonsful wholemeal flour
1 loosely-beaten egg
1 finely-chopped and gently-fried onion
50g (2 oz.) grated cheese
1 tablespoonful water
1 tablespoonful milk
salt, pepper and fresh green herbs to taste
breadcrumbs
oil to fry

Mix the oats with the flour, the milk, the water, the egg, the cheese, the onion and the chopped herbs, e.g., chives, parsley, celery tops. Season with salt and pepper to taste.

Make four nice round flat cakes out of the mixture, coat them with breadcrumbs and fry them in a little hot oil for ten minutes or until the oatcakes are golden-brown and done.

Serve with a potato salad or a pulse salad.

Oatcakes with Vegetables

These flat oatcakes are served as a main dish, accompanied with a salad of the season.

For four people we will need:

200g (7 oz.) oats
2 large onions
3 large leeks
1 large or several small carrots
a piece of celeriac or some celery tops
3 tablespoonsful oil
some boiling water
rosemary, salt and pepper to taste
1 egg

Chop up and grate the vegetables quite small and fry them gently in the hot oil, with the rosemary and the pepper until they are soft but not brown. Add 2 cupsful of boiling water and the oats. Boil for five minutes, stirring all the time, pour out onto a plate and spread the 'porridge' out one finger thick. Leave it to cool. Shape nice little cakes, coat them with the loosely beaten egg and fry them golden-brown in some hot oil.

Serve them hot with a salad.

Muesli with Oats

8 tablespoonsful oatflakes
1 glass milk
3 tablespoonsful raisins
3 apples
½ cupful finely-chopped nuts

1 banana
the juice and grated skin of 1 lemon
honey for sweetening

Soak the oatflakes, the raisins and the grated lemon skin overnight in one glass of milk.

The next morning add the freshly-grated apples, the chopped nuts, the sliced banana, the juice of the lemon and honey to taste.

Any other fresh fruit may be added.

Serve this fresh, delicious and wholesome for breakfast.

This quantity will serve four average eaters.

If desired, one may add a spoonful of cream, but this is certainly not essential. The oats may also be soaked in water and half a glass of thin cream be added just before serving the next morning.

Muesli with Oats and Orange Juice

This type of muesli needs only a short soaking time and can therefore be prepared on the same day.

125g (4½ oz.) oats
1 litre (1¾ pt.) yogurt
6 tablespoonsful honey
2 dcl (7 fl. oz.) orange juice
50g (2 oz.) finely-chopped nuts

Soak the nuts in the yogurt for one hour only and add the honey, the orange juice and the nuts just before serving.

Serve this dessert as cold as possible, preferably after a main course of pulses, as the yogurt will help the body to absorb the vegetable proteins of the pulses.

Omelette with Oats

25g (1 oz.) oats
4 tablespoonsful water
4 eggs
salt and pepper
oil or margarine for frying

2 tablespoonsful finely-chopped fresh herbs, such as parsley, chervil, chives, dill, etc.

Soak the oats in the water for one hour. Loosely beat the eggs with a little salt. Add the oats and most of the freshly-chopped garden herbs.

Melt the margarine or heat the oil in a frying pan. Pour the egg mixture into the hot oil.

Use a spoon to push the cooked part of the omelette away from the sides and allow the uncooked egg to get all over the pan.

Continue until the omelette is completely cooked. Sprinkle the remaining herbs on top and serve the omelette hot with a crisp, green salad.

11
Maize

Maize or ZEA MAYS is a tall annual grain.

In this country it is grown almost exclusively for cattle feeding purposes. Chickens especially are very fond of maize and in popular speech maize is more or less identical to chicken feed.

It seems to occur to very few people that the same 'chicken feed' also provides us with cornflour, which is well known and much used, and maize oil, which has recently become very popular.

In this cookery book, however, we do not want to waste our time talking about cornflour, a product which is rich in carbohydrates and precious little else, or even about maize oil, excellent though it is with its many polyunsaturated fats.

In this chapter we want to talk about the maize ear, freshly picked from the plant and about maize flour, a pleasant addition to our grain products.

Concerning maize ears: they should be young, not too ripe as the kernels will turn hard and floury with age. When picked at the right time, maize kernels are sweet, tender and juicy, a little similar to very young, fresh garden peas.

Fresh maize ears can be cooked whole in water in a large saucepan, or the kernel can be removed from the ear with a fork and cooked in a little water. Maize flour is presently available in most health stores and can be cooked into a wholesome thick porridge with just a little water and some salt. This porridge, which combines well with almost every savoury or sweet food, is well known in southern European countries under the name of 'Polenta', and tastes quite different and makes a change from the other grains. Maize, however, with only a maximum of 10 per cent in vegetable proteins and very few trace minerals and vitamins, can not be considered a champion among the grains.

Polenta

A thick polenta plays the same role in many regions of Italy as the potato does in our northerly countries: a main dish that is eaten with some vegetables and a meat dish.

Polenta is more versatile than the potato, as it can also be eaten as a dessert, when some stewed or fresh fruit is served with it.

Sweetened with honey it makes a delicious porridge.

In short, there are plenty of possibilities with this neutral tasting dish. For four persons we need:

300g (11 oz.) maize meal
¼ litre (½ pt.) water
a pinch of salt

Bring the water to the boil, add the salt and sprinkle the maize meal into the boiling water, stirring all the time. Simmer this porridge very gently for ten minutes, but beware of burning.

Continuous stirring can prevent this.

Serve the polenta as hot as possible.

Polenta with Tomatoes and Mushrooms

Make a polenta as described above.
Then make a sauce:

300g (11 oz.) ripe tomatoes
200g (7 oz.) fresh mushrooms
2 large onions
oil, salt and rosemary

Chop the onions finely and gently fry them, until they are soft. Add

the peeled and sliced tomatoes. Season to taste with the salt and
the rosemary and add the sliced mushrooms shortly before serving.
  Simmer for a few minutes only, taking care not to over-cook the
mushrooms.
  Serve this sauce piping hot with polenta.

Maize Porridge

A maize porridge, made of maize grits, may be eaten with savoury
or sweet foods, just like a polenta.
  Maize porridge improves if the grits are briefly toasted in a little oil
in a heavy saucepan.
  Take:

300g (11 oz.) maize grits
¼ litre (½ pt.) water
a pinch of salt

Sprinkle the grits into boiling, salted water and cook for fifteen
minutes.

Maize and Vegetable Dish

400g (14 oz.) fresh maize kernels
2 tablespoonsful oil
2 onions
1 red sweet pepper
4 tomatoes
salt and pepper to taste
4 eggs
parsley

Cook the fresh maize kernels in a little water. Fry the finely-
chopped onions and the diced peppers, until they are soft but not
brown. Add the peeled, sliced tomatoes and season the vegetables
with salt and pepper to taste.
  Strain the cooked maize kernels well and add them to the onion
and pepper mixture. Mix well, and place in a flat ovenware dish.
  Using a small ladle, make four depressions in the vegetable layer
and break an egg into each depression. Sprinkle a little salt and

pepper on each egg and place the dish into a hot oven to thoroughly heat the dish and cook the eggs.

Garnish with freshly-picked, chopped parsley just before serving and serve this filling dish with mashed potatoes, cooked rice or buckwheat.

Maize Salad

200g (7 oz.) fresh maize kernels
200g (7 oz.) unpolished rice
50g (2 oz.) raisins
1 large carrot
50g (2 oz.) walnuts
a few lettuce leaves
a dressing of 3 tablespoonsful oil, juice of 1 lemon, sea salt
**   and freshly chopped parsley and/or dill**

Cook the rice in the usual way or use some left over from the previous day. Cook the raisins a little to make them swell, strain them well.

Cook the maize kernels in a little water.

Grate the carrot and sprinkle some lemon over it. Make a dressing of the oil, the lemon juice, a little sea salt and some fresh herbs.

Mix all the ingredients thoroughly with the dressing before placing the salad in a salad bowl lined with washed and dried lettuce leaves.

Sprinkle the finely-chopped nuts on the top and serve this delicious salad with fried cheese slices or an omelette.

12
Sesame Seed

Sesame seed is a seed of almost mystical powers.

It strengthens the spirit and opens it up to good and noble thoughts. We use sesame as an oil or simply eat the seeds.

The seeds, more so than the oil, possess amazing powers that not only rejuvenate the spirit but also keep the body young and healthy.

Sesame seed is very rich in vegetable protein and tastes very good with most vegetables and in sandwiches.

In order to fully enjoy the flavour of the sesame seed, it must be toasted in a little oil over a low fire, as it has little taste if left untoasted. Toasted, however, it changes into a delicacy, and becomes crisp with the taste of fragrant nuts.

Most health stores sell sesame seed, toasted as well as untoasted.

When and how do we use sesame seed?

We could simply sprinkle some freshly-toasted sesame seed on a buttered slice of brown bread, with or without a little marmite to add to the taste.

We can stir some toasted sesame seed into a jar of honey. It transforms the honey into something very special, more fragrant and delicious than before as well as wholesome and healthy.

Sesame seed is ideally suited to be added to any cooked green vegetable, to soups, sauces and sprinkled over a green salad.

We could also mix a handful of untoasted sesame seeds through our bread dough, which will then delight everyone.

Finally there is 'gomasio', a macrobiotic herb salt, made of sesame seed and sea salt, that we add to soups and sauces for seasoning. It gives our food an extra fragrant strength. Gomasio can be eaten in sandwiches, too. Few recipes mention sesame, but why not experiment a little? It has such a delightful nutty taste that few people can resist it. It grows on one and can easily become a very good and healthy habit!

Sesame seed has been known as a spice for many centuries. We come across it in Babylonion mythology when Mardoek, the son of the gods, drank a herbal wine with sesame seed to gather strength before he started the creation of the earth.

Sesame Seed Croquettes
For four people:
4 cupsful boiled rice, millet or buckwheat
½ cupful grated cheese
½ cupful finely chopped green garden herbs
½ cupful toasted sesame seed
some wholemeal flour
water
sea salt

Knead all the ingredients except the wholemeal flour into a supple dough and make little croquettes. Roll them through the wholemeal flour and fry them golden-brown in a frying pan, or deep fry.

Carrot and Sesame Salad
This is a wholesome winter salad which becomes extra nourishing because of the added sesame seed. Prepare as shortly before serving as possible.

3 large carrots
100g (4 oz.) sesame seed
2 tablespoonsful sunflower oil
½ lemon
1 cupful yogurt or sour cream
1 teaspoonful honey

Toast the sesame seeds carefully in a little oil until they are crisp and taste like nuts. Leave them to cool and meanwhile grate the washed carrots, finely or coarsely as desired. Mix the grated carrot with the sesame seed.

Make a dressing of the honey, the yogurt, the juice of half a lemon and the oil.

The best result is obtained if the honey is mixed thoroughly with the oil, then the lemon juice is added and finally the yogurt or sour cream.

Sesame Sauce

4 tablespoonsful tamari (a soy extract)
1 cupful sesame seed per person
1 cupful finely-chopped water cress

Toast the sesame seed in a dry saucepan, crush it in a mortar until it becomes slightly oily. Stir in the tamari and finally the water cress. An excellent sauce to go with unpolished rice or millet.

13

Rice

Rice is a member of the great grain and grass family. It derives its English name from the Latin, ORYZA SATIVA.

Although we import most of our rice from Asia and South America, rice will occasionally grow in Europe as well, notably in the wet parts of southern France and southern Italy. Rice needs a lot of water, as well as plenty of sunshine and warmth, which explains why this country, wet though it may be, is unsuitable for rice growing.

The foreign origin of rice explains why we find only the odd one or two recipes in old cookery books mentioning rice. If they do, it is usually a recipe for rice pudding, with or without currants and saffron. This dish, however, was held in such high esteem that it served to make the mountains that surround the land of Cockaigne. Only people who could eat themselves through the mountains of rice pudding, could enter this country of plenty.

At the beginning of this century, mainly because the ties with the colonies became firmer, more and more rice dishes appeared in British kitchens and since World War II, the absence of rice from our menu would be unthinkable and be considered disastrous.

Unfortunately, though, we usually eat the wrong sort of rice, i.e., polished, which is very high in carbohydrates and has no vitamins or trace minerals to speak of. This is strange, really, as we should all know better.

The discovery of vitamin B1 is entirely due to the polish of rice. Dr. Eykman, a Dutch medical doctor who discovered it, was awarded a Nobel Prize for it.

The story is a simple one. This doctor, who had been studying the possible causes of beri-beri, went on a journey and on his return to the hospital in Batavia (now Jakarta, Indonesia) he found that the hospital chickens seemed to make the same strange unco-ordinated movements as sufferers from the much-feared beri-beri disease.

When he investigated he found out that they had been fed on unpolished rice from the hospital kitchens during his absence, instead of their usual diet of unpolished rice.

The actual silvery polish of the rice, which is removed in the polishing process, apparently contained something that could not only cure, but even prevent beri-beri. Thus vitamin B1 was discovered.

Therefore it goes without saying that this cookery book presumes the use of brown, unpolished rice, half-polished rice if need be, but never the white, polished· vitamin-lacking variety, when rice is mentioned. In this book we try to compose a diet which is as healthy and complete as possible. Brown rice has to cook slightly longer than the peeled, polished and bleached kind, but the result is worth the effort.

Unpolished Rice
For four people:

4 cupsful brown, unpolished rice
8 cupsful water
a little sea salt to taste

Put the rice in a large sieve and wash it thoroughly under running cold water, stirring all the time.

Place it in a heavy saucepan, add the water and the salt. Bring to the boil and leave to boil for approximately seven minutes without covering. Skim, stir through the rice and cover. Leave to simmer over a very low fire (or wrapped in a blanket) for at least one hour, or until done.

Half-Polished Rice

There are people who have to get used to the idea of eating the wholesome natural rice and there are those who have a weak stomach, and last but not least there are the hurriers, who never allow themselves time to wait for their rice for one, whole hour.

For all those people we suggest the use of half-polished rice, which is not quite so strong in taste, is more easily digested and is cooked in fifteen minutes.

For four people:

4 cupsful half-polished rice
6 cupsful water
a little sea salt

Wash the rice under the running tap, then put it in a heavy saucepan on the stove with the water and salt and bring it to the boil. Cover and cook the rice over a low fire in fifteen minutes, or until dry and done.

Rice can be served with almost every vegetable and sauce, and here are some ideas to set you experimenting, as the possibilities are endless for a creative cook.

Rice with Fried Banana

For four people:

4 cupsful boiled rice
4 small onions
2 bananas
2 eggs
4 tablespoonsful sunflower oil
a little sea salt

Fry the finely-chopped onions in some oil until they are golden-brown and add the boiled rice. Season to taste with sea salt and fresh garden herbs of one's own choice. Stir and heat thoroughly.

Meanwhile, fry the bananas, that have been cut length-wise, in one frying pan and make an omelette of the two eggs in another.

Put the steaming hot rice on a heated flat serving dish and garnish the dish with the fried bananas and strips of omelette. If desired, serve with a sweet tomato sauce.

Chinese Rice Dish

4 cupsful boiled unpolished rice
3 finely-chopped onions
3 tablespoonsful sunflower oil
2 eggs
sea salt
nutmeg
2 tablespoonsful tamari (a soy extract)

Fry the onions in the oil and add the boiled rice. Stir gently and heat thoroughly. Loosely beat the egg, add the salt, the nutmeg and the tamari and stir it very carefully into the rice and onion mixture.

Leave it to set over a low heat or put it in an ovenware dish into the oven and leave it to brown.

A green salad will complete this nourishing main course.

Savoury Rice and Cheese Cakes
For four people:

2 cupsful boiled brown rice
2 cupsful baker's cheese (quark)
½ cupful grated nuts
the juice of 1 lemon
100g (4 oz.) wholemeal flour
1 egg
milk
parsley
salt and spices to taste (cumin seed tastes good!)

Mix all the ingredients thoroughly together in a large bowl and make the mixture into flat round cakes of approximately half an inch thick. Fry these cakes in a little oil, or bake them in the oven on a well-oiled baking sheet.

Serve these cheese cakes hot and fragrant straight from the oven as a delicious surprise at teatime, or as a main course. In the latter case they should be preceded by a savoury soup and followed by a fruit salad.

Rice Salad

One might not think of it, but a little dry, boiled rice added to a salad, improves the taste of that salad. It seems to strike a perfect balance with the crispness of the spicy tasting greens.

For four people:

2 cupsful boiled rice
4 cupsful mixed, uncooked vegetables such as endive,
carrots, celeriac etc.

Chop up or grate the vegetables and mix them with the rice. Make a dressing of:

2 tablespoonsful sunflower oil
the juice of one lemon
a little tamari
parsley to taste

Pour the dressing over the salad and mix gently and thoroughly. Garnish this salad with crisp young radishes and hard-boiled, halved eggs.

Rice and Nut Dish

4 cupsful boiled rice
150g (5 oz.) bread-crumbs
120g (4½ oz.) chopped, mixed nuts
juice of 1 lemon
chopped celery greens

Mix all the ingredients together and put them in a buttered ovenware dish. Sprinkle a few breadcrumbs on the top and add a few small knobs of butter. Heat thoroughly in a moderately warm oven. Serve immediately.

Rice and Apricot Salad

2 cupsful unpolished rice
60g (2 oz.) dried, soaked apricots
60g (2 oz.) chopped nuts
2 onions
1 clove of garlic
1 large carrot
a piece of ginger root
parsley
150g (5 oz.) baker's cheese (quark)
juice of 1 lemon
1 tablespoonful vinegar
4 tablespoonsful raisins
sea salt to taste

Boil the rice in salted water. After thirty minutes add the cut-up apricots in their soaking water to the rice. Meanwhile fry the onion, the garlic, the ginger root and the carrot, all finely chopped.

Add this to the rice as well and continue to cook until the mixture is dry and done.

Finally add the lemon juice, the wine vinegar, the chopped nuts, the parsley, the raisins and the baker's cheese and carefully mix everything together.

Chill this dish thoroughly and serve it cold.

Rice and Vegetable Pie

200g (7 oz.) wholemeal flour
sea salt
3 tablespoonsful vegetable oil
a little water
2 cupsful boiled rice
2 onions
100g (4 oz.) cheese
100g (4 oz.) edible mushrooms
2 cupsful vegetables of the season (e.g. cucumber, tomato,
    beans, cabbage, fresh wild vegetables)

Make a nice springy dough of the wholemeal flour, the oil, a little water and some salt.

Line a pie dish with it.

Fry the finely-chopped onions and the sliced mushrooms in a little oil and add the other vegetables. Fill the pie with a layer of rice, a layer of fried vegetables, a layer of cheese (sliced or grated), rice again, more vegetables and finally the remainder of the cheese.

Put it in the oven for approximately thirty-five minutes or until golden-brown and done. Serve immediately with a green, crisp salad. Freshly picked dandelion leaves taste excellent with this dish.

Rice Soufflé

3 eggs
3/8 litre (¾ pt.) cream
salt, pepper, nutmeg to taste
3 tablespoonsful finely chopped onion
3 tablespoonsful finely chopped parsley
8 hard-boiled eggs
500g (1 lb) boiled rice
4 tablespoonsful grated cheese
a knob of butter

Mix the loosely-beaten eggs with the cream, the parsley and the fried onion. Season it with salt, pepper and nutmeg.

Mix the boiled rice gently with the sliced boiled eggs and fold in the cream mixture.

Put it in a buttered ovenware dish, cover it with grated cheese and a few small knobs of butter. Bake this SOUFFLÉ in an oven of 250°C (500°F Gas Mark 8) for approximately thirty minutes.

14

Rye

Rye, with its Latin name of SECALE CEREALE, is one of the grains that grow well on sandy soils. It contains a similar 10 per cent vegetable protein to most other grains, but, unfortunately, rye is not popular in this country. There are very few indigenous rye recipes. It is sometimes used in gingerbread and, of course, rye is made into ryebread.

Rye Bread

Rye bread is made in the same way as other breads.

It can be made with yeast or with leaven, but whole rye flour is very heavy and will hardly rise. Therefore, we usually make a lighter rye bread by mixing equal quantities of rye flour and wholemeal flour.

The result is a delicious, more easily digestible loaf of rye bread.

Kruska of Rye Flour

2 tablespoonsful coarsely ground whole rye flour
2 tablespoonsful coarsely ground wholemeal flour
2 tablespoonsful porridge oats
2 tablespoonsful ground millet

2 tablespoonsful barley
2 tablespoonsful raisins
½ litre (¾ pt.) water

Mix all the ingredients thoroughly together, bring to the boil and simmer for five minutes.

Put the covered saucepan in a cooking box (hay-box) or wrap it in a blanket, or pillows and leave it to cook and dry in approximately one hour.

Kruska is eaten as hot as possible with a little milk or some stewed fresh fruit.

It is a nutritious and delightful dish, which is ideally suited to be eaten after a main course soup with vegetables or pulses.

15

Wheat

Wheat, named TRICIUM in Latin, is the most popular and well-known grain in our part of the world.

There are many different varieties of TRICIUM, but in this country TRICIUM AESTIVIUM is usually grown.

This type of wheat likes heavy, rich soil and will grow considerably better on clay than on sandy soils.

Like most other grains, the full wheat grain contents a fairly high percentage of vegetable protein, namely 11 per cent, as well as a very high level of carbohydrates. It also contains some very important trace minerals and vitamins.

The use of white flour, or bread made of white flour, considerably reduces the quantity of vitamins, vitamin B among others, and of trace minerals, such as iron, phosphorus and calcium.

The use of white flour is a total folly and a waste, as the best parts of the grain are taken out, thrown away or are being used for fodder.

It stands to reason that this cookery book, which advocates a healthy and full, natural diet, means wholemeal flour at all times.

However, there is more to wholemeal flour. A grain of wheat lives and breathes. A whole grain can keep its good and healthy qualities for a long, long time. Once ground, however, the unity of the grain has been broken and its good qualities quickly diminish. Therefore good wholemeal flour is freshly-ground wholemeal flour.

This is available at all good reputable Health stores, but why not grind one's own? It is true, one needs to buy a special hand mill, which is altogether different from the ordinary coffee grinder. But why not? The taste of the flour and the bread made with it, is a taste not easily forgotten.

Whichever way one uses to obtain freshly-ground flour, its value in the alternative kitchen cannot be disputed.

It is indispensable as a binder of soups and sauces, as a main ingredient of pancakes and porridge and last, but by no means least, as the main ingredient of bread.

We consider this of such importance that we included a separate chapter on bread, which will tell all the delicious secrets.

Cooked Wheat Grain

The whole grain of wheat, provided it is cooked, may be used to replace rice. The actual cooking is very simple, but it takes a little more time. For the best result the grain should be left to soak overnight.
Take:

300g (11 oz.) whole grains of wheat
6 dcl (21 fl. oz.) water
salt to taste

Soak the grains in the water overnight. The next morning bring them to the boil, stirring constantly.

Boil for five minutes and keep stirring.

Leave the wheat to get dry and done in 1½ hours, in a cooking box or over a very, very low heat.

Beware of burning, though.

Wheat with Vegetables and Nuts

300g (11 oz.) whole wheat grains
6 dcl (21 fl. oz.) water
2 onions
2 large onions

a cupful of chopped nuts
oil, salt, pepper and fresh herbs

Boil the wheat as described in the recipe above.

Meanwhile gently fry the finely chopped onions and grated carrots in a little hot oil. Mix them through the hot rice, season it with salt, pepper and freshly chopped garden herbs. Finally mix in the finely-chopped nuts.

Serve this dish hot with a green salad.

Wheat with Honey and Raisins

This is a nutritious dessert which can be served after a light main course.

Soak overnight:

300g (11 oz.) wheat grains
200g (7 oz.) raisins
7½ dcl (25 fl. oz.) water

Bring all the ingredients to the boil and cook it, as described in the recipes above, until it is dry and done. Serve this dish with molten honey or stir in a large tablespoonful of honey just before serving.

Chocolate Pudding with Wholemeal Flour

¾ litre (1 pt.) strong cocoa, made with equal quantities of milk and water
70g (2½ oz.) wholemeal flour
50g (2 oz.) raisins
honey to taste

Make a very strong cocoa of equal quantities of water and milk.

Meanwhile toast the wholemeal flour in a heavy saucepan, but do not brown. Mix this with a little cocoa in a cup, add the raisins and pour this mixture into the boiling cocoa.

Simmer this pudding on a low fire for fifteen minutes, until thick and cooked. Keep stirring constantly. Sweeten with honey according to taste. Pour the chocolate pudding into a pudding dish and sprinkle some chopped nuts or toasted oat flakes on the top for decoration.

Semolina Pudding with Toasted Almonds

¾ litre (1 pt.) milk
70g (2½ oz.) semolina
1 egg
50g (2 oz.) toasted almond flakes
honey or sugar to taste

Bring the milk to the boil. Sprinkle the semolina into the boiling milk and cook the semolina pudding for approximately five minutes, stirring all the time. Stir in the almond flakes and remove the saucepan from the heat. Stir the loosely-beaten egg into the semolina pudding. Replace the saucepan on the fire until the mixture has thickened nicely.

Sweeten to taste with honey or brown sugar and pour the pudding into a pudding dish.

Wholemeal Pastry
This recipe is enough to fill a ovenware dish or a pie dish of 18-20cm (7-8 inches).

Take:

150g (5 oz.) wholemeal flour
3 tablespoonsful sunflower oil
salt
a little loosely beaten egg
water
a few drops of lemon juice

Put the flour, the oil and a little salt in a large bowl and knead into a smooth dough, using a little cold water when necessary. A few drops of lemon juice will help to make the dough lighter and crisper. When the dough is smooth, it is rolled out on a floured board, cloth or work top. It should be about 1½cm (½ inch) thick when rolled out completely.

Butter a pie dish or cake tin, line it carefully with the pastry and fill it. The pie can be covered with the remaining dough, which is rolled out once more to fit the top of the pie dish. Carefully cover the pie, brush it with some loosely beaten egg and cut a cross-shape in the middle of the pastry-lid to let out the air and the cooking juices. The pie is placed in a hot oven (200°C/400°F Gas Mark 6) for fifteen minutes, then the heat is reduced to 175°C (350°F/Gas Mark 4) and the pie is baked for half an hour.

Serve piping hot!

Savoury Pie Filling

2 onions
2 leeks
3 tomatoes
1 green sweet pepper
1 large carrot
parsley, chives, salt, pepper and oil
1 cupful cooked peas, maize or green beans

Gently fry the onions and the leeks in a little oil, add the chopped pepper, the grated carrot and finally the peeled and sliced tomatoes. Season the mixture with salt and pepper, add freshly-chopped parsley and chives to taste and finally mix in the cup of cooked vegetables. Use this mixture to fill a pie, and serve it hot as a main dish (see above recipe).

Prune Pie

300g (11 oz.) dried prunes
cinnamon to taste
honey if desired

Soak the prunes overnight, de-stone them and cook them over a low heat till they are soft, but not mashy. Season them with cinnamon and a little honey to taste. Strain them thoroughly and use them to fill a pie.

Apple Pie

700g (1½ lb) cooking apples
100g (4 oz.) raisins
cinnamon, lemon juice and honey to taste

Fill the pie with the peeled and chopped apples and the soaked, but well-drained raisins. Put some lemon juice, cinnamon and honey over this mixture and cover the pie with strips of left-over dough, making a trellis-work.

Bake as described in the 'Wholemeal Pastry' recipe.

This pie can be eaten hot from the oven with cream, or cold. Do not leave too long, as the pie may become soggy, which is a waste of a delicious, traditional dessert.

Wholemeal Soup with Orache

1 litre (1¾ pt.) vegetable broth
1 tablespoonful vegetable oil
3 tablespoonsful freshly ground wholemeal flour
1 onion
a generous bunch of freshly picked Orache (approximately 150g 5 oz.) some very finely chopped celery tops.

Heat the oil in a large, heavy saucepan, add and gently fry the finely-chopped onion and gradually add the flour, stirring all the time.

When the mixture has turned into a lovely golden-brown, take a whisk, add the hot vegetable broth and beat briskly until the soup is smooth and fragrant. Simmer for a few minutes before adding the finely chopped orache and celery tops. Boil for one to two minutes more and serve immediately.

Semolina and Apple Pudding

This is a recipe which can be served with a filling pulse soup, as an ENTRÉE or sweet.

1 litre (1¾ pt.) milk
100g (4 oz.) semolina
sugar or honey
lemon peel
4 large apples
farina to thicken

Bring the milk and the lemon peel to the boil and stir the semolina into the boiling milk. Cook the semolina for five minutes, stirring all the time and sweeten it to taste with sugar or honey. Pour the pudding into a pudding dish and leave it to cool.

Meanwhile, peel the apples and core them. Cut them in half. Cook them in some water and lemon juice, but do not overcook and break them.

Scoop them out of the fluid and place them on top of the cooled semolina pudding.

Pour a little of the fluid over the top, after having thickened it with a little farina.

Serve this pudding very cold.

16

Bread

We all know it: bread, like so many other things, is no longer what it used to be. Technology, which rules our lives to an ever increasing extent, has got hold of our daily bread. It has turned a piece of beautiful craftsmanship into a piece of tasteless, colourless factory work.

An ever growing number of people are getting so fed up with this bleached, de-naturalized, spoiled bread, that they have started to make their own. Quite an adventure at first, but definitely worth the effort, for the end result is so infinitely more fragrant, tastier, healthier and better than the cottonwool bread of the factory.

It is, however, a job of work that takes time, not suitable for people in a hurry. Especially, if we make bread with home-made leaven, which has many advantages over factory-made yeast. Not only do we know exactly what ingredients we used, which is more than we can say of the yeast, but also, we know that leaven helps the body absorb the vegetable proteins. All the precious trace minerals of the wheat grain are preserved when leaven is being used.

The making of leaven is not difficult, but it requires patience again. One needs six days, before one can begin to make bread.

Leaven

Mix three tablespoonsful of wholemeal flour and a little lukewarm water into a paste. Cover the mixture and put it in a lukewarm place. After three days it will begin to bubble and to ferment. Time to add a little more water and a little more flour. Give it a good stir and repeat this procedure for two days.

Should we want to do it in exactly the right way, we should stir and add water and flour early in the morning and at night, but once only will do the job as well.

Six days after we started our leaven is ready for use and there should be enough to make two 500g (1 lb) loaves of wholemeal flour, or wholemeal mixed with rye, some buckwheat or a handful of millet.

Bread made with Leaven

1 kg (2 lb) wholemeal flour, or a mixture of wholemeal and rye, wholemeal and buckwheat or wholemeal and millet
1 cupful vegetable oil (may be left out, if desired)
1 cupful homemade leaven
½ litre (¾ pt.) lukewarm water
sea salt to taste

Put the flour in a large bowl and make a depression in the middle. Fill this with the oil, the leaven, a little sea salt and the lukewarm water. Mix the ingredients together and start kneading the dough with the kneading-hooks of an electric mixer or better still, with clean hands. Go on kneading for at least fifteen minutes. The dough will feel silky, smooth and supple when it is ready. Put the dough in the bowl, cover it with a moist cloth and leave it to rise in a warm place for a few hours. A whole night is even better.

Knead it through once more and divide it over two well-greased bread tins. However, do not forget to keep a piece of the dough the size of a large potato. Place this in a well-covered bowl and keep it in the refrigerator. It will keep for two to three weeks. Before further use, the leaven is put in a warm place again and mixed with more flour and water for three successive days. It will then be ready for use once more.

In some parts of Europe a young bride is given a piece of leaven by her mother on her wedding day. The idea is that she can start baking bread in her new house with old leaven, which is supposed to be superior to new.

But, back to our loaves!

They are in the tins now and can be left to rise for an hour if desired, though many bakers put them straight into the oven.

The oven must be preheated to 240°C (450°F/Gas Mark 8).

The bread will be cooked through in thirty minutes and can be taken from the oven. It should immediately be turned out of the tins onto a cake rack to cool.

Bread made with Yeast

1 kg (2 lb) flour
40g (2 oz.) yeast
1 cupful oil (if desired)
½ litre (¾ pt.) milk or water
sea salt to taste

We get our fresh yeast from the baker's.

As we usually buy more than we need, it is practical to know how to keep the remainder of the yeast fresh. Press the yeast into the bottom of a glass, then put the glass upside down into a bowl of water so that no air can get at it. Store it in a dark, cool place e.g. the refrigerator or a cellar and the yeast will stay 'alive' for approximately three weeks.

We need 40g (2 oz.) of baker's yeast to 1 kg of flour.

Take a little lukewarm milk and dissolve the yeast, stirring it into a smooth paste. Leave this to rise in a warm place for thirty minutes. Put the flour in a large bowl, make a depression in the middle and fill it with the yeast/milk mixture, the oil, some sea salt and the remaining milk or water, or even a mixture of both. We follow the preparation of bread with leaven closely, for now we mix all the ingredients together and start kneading, preferably by hand, but the kneading-hooks of the mixer can also do a good job. When the dough is supple and smooth to the touch, it is left to rise for forty-five minutes, covered with a cloth in a slightly warm place.

Knead through once more and roll the dough out on a work top.

Cut the sheet of dough in half and roll up each half and put them in the well-greased bread tins.

Leave them, covered, to rise for another forty-five minutes. Pre-heat the oven to 240°C (450°F/Gas Mark 8) and bake the loaves in thirty minutes.

Yeast bread, like leaven bread, can be made with wholemeal flour or wholemeal flour mixed with rye flour, millet, buckwheat flour, a little sesame seed, currants or raisins.

New combinations are bound to be discovered when baking becomes a regular thing. There are so many possibilities.

When we make the dough slightly firm, we can bake the loaves on a baking sheet, without the use of tins. We can make a round loaf, or a plaited loaf, made with three equal strips of dough or we can try a french loaf.

Baking bread becomes one of the creative ways of expressing oneself to many a housewife.

A kind of hobby with a delicious end-result!

17

Sauces

Sauces can turn any dull dish into a festive one. They are a perfect solution when we have some left-over rice, pulse or millet.

They give a different taste to our salads and they turn ordinary vegetables like endive, cabbage or leeks into a gourmet dish.

In short, sauces are wonderful! And a good cook can do wonders with them! Most dishes that cry out for a sauce usually give the recipe for a sauce as well. However, cooking should not be dull, it should be a never-ending adventure, a delicious discovery of new possibilities. To help you along we have included a short chapter on simple, delicious sauces that are easy to make. We have given serving suggestions for most recipes, but who is stopping you from trying out something different!

Apple and Horseradish Sauce

Apple sauce is delicious over beetroots and cooked red cabbage, but red kidney beans and lentils appreciate the taste of apples as well. The apple sauce turns pulse dishes into a lighter, better food.

Apples combine well with horseradish. You will need:

4 firm cooking apples (Bramleys)
1 small spoonful sunflower oil

4 tablespoonsful water
¼ tablespoonful lemon juice
a little lemon peel, grated
1 small cupful grated horseradish

Peel, quarter and core the apples. Cut each quarter in half again and gently stew the apple in the oil until they are cooked but not brown. Add the water, the lemon juice, the lemon peel and the grated horseradish. Stir well, heat thoroughly and pass the sauce through a sieve. Serve it hot with lentils, red kidney beans or beetroots.

A little fresh finely-chopped lemon balm is an extra.

Apple and Sour Cream Sauce

4 apples
1 small spoonful sunflower oil
¼ litre (½ pt.) sour cream or yogurt
1 teaspoonful Marmite
a little garlic to taste

Peel, quarter and core the apples. Stew them in the oil until they are done. Mash them with a fork and stir in the sour cream and the Marmite. Add a little garlic juice to taste, if desired.

Serve hot with rice or haricot beans.

Apple and Ginger Sauce

4 apples
½ cupful water
4 pieces of stem ginger
1 tablespoonful soy oil
honey and lemon juice to taste

Peel, quarter and core the apples. Cook them in the water until they are soft and mashy. Meanwhile finely chop up the ginger and add it to the stewed apples together with the soy oil. Beat the sauce until it is light and frothy. Add honey and a little lemon juice to taste.

It is difficult to give exact quantities as this depends mainly on the size and the type of apples used.

This tangy sauce tastes well with lentils or red kidney beans, but it goes well with stewed red cabbage too.

Green Herbs and Egg Sauce

2 hard-boiled eggs
1 raw egg yolk
salt and pepper to taste
1 dcl (3½ fl. oz.) oil
the juice of 1 lemon or a tablespoonful vinegar
1 dcl (3½ fl. oz.) yogurt
4 tablespoonsful finely-chopped fresh green garden herbs,
**   such as chives, dill, parsley, garden-cress, chervil.**

Pass the hard-boiled eggs through a sieve and mix them with the raw egg yolk. Season the mixture with salt and pepper to taste.

Slowly add the oil and the vinegar (or lemon juice), stirring all the time. When the sauce has thickened and is nice and smooth the yogurt and the herbs may be added.

A delicious sauce over hard-boiled egg, or as a dressing for a large mixed salad. It will taste very good with asparagus.

Baker's Cheese (quark) Sauce

125g (4½ oz.) baker's Cheese (also called skim milk
**   cheese or quark)**
a little milk
½ cupful finely chopped fresh green garden herbs

Cream the baker's cheese with some milk and beat it into a smooth sauce. Add the herbs, such as garden cress, parsley, chervil, lovage, celery tops, etc., and stir them in.

Very good with all kinds of potato dishes, also excellent with cucumber and tomato.

Mint Sauce
An old favourite, but worth including on the list of sauces.

**2 tablespoonsful of very finely chopped mint (peppermint
   or spearmint)**
the juice of 1 lemon
2 tablespoonsful water
3 tablespoonsful brown sugar

Stir all the ingredients together and leave this sauce for at least
twenty minutes before using it. The fragrance of the mint will need
a little time to mix with the other ingredients.
 Serve this sweet and sour sauce with pulse for a change, like
beans and lentils or serve it with cooked rice and buckwheat.

18
Nuts

Nut Mayonnaise

Mix a tablespoonful of nut paste; almond, hazelnut or walnut, with a little water into a thick sauce. Add ¼ litre (½ pt.) of sunflower oil gradually, stirring all the time.

Add the juice of a lemon and finally some finely chopped marjoram, dill and horseradish.

Nut Mayonnaise with Tomato Purée

Make a nut mayonnaise as described above but leave out the herbs and add a little garlic powder and a few spoonsful of tomato PURÉE instead.

Nut Mayonnaise with Gherkins

Make a nut mayonnaise as above and finally add some finely chopped or sliced gherkins.

Use this mayonnaise as a dressing for all types of salad.

Toasted Almond Dish

Are you planning a dinner party? Spoil your guests and treat them to this delicious toasted almond dish.

It is a fragrant and delicate-tasting dish, which is so nutritious that no ENTRÉE or dessert are necessary. Just a nice miso sauce with onions to go with it. An oven, however, is essential for this dish. For four large (and five ordinary) eaters, we need:

100g (4 oz.) peeled almonds
2 slices brown bread, in crumbs
2 tablespoonsful buckwheat, cooked
1 dcl (3½ fl. oz.) vegetable broth
25g (1 oz.) sunflower oil
1 cupful finely chopped onion
1 cupful finely chopped carrot
½ cupful finely sliced mushrooms
1 tablespoonful finely chopped parsley with a little
   marjoram, sweet basil and thyme
1 loosely beaten egg

Mix all the ingredients together into an even thick mixture. Place in a well-greased ovenware dish, or baking tin. Place in a moderate oven and cook for one hour or until it is done. Serve it straight from the oven with a miso sauce with onion.

Miso Sauce

4 tablespoonsful miso (a paste of soya and sea salt)
3 dcl (10½ fl. oz.) water
2 tablespoonsful sunflower oil
1 finely chopped onion
2 tablespoonsful brown rice flour
1 large piece of ginger root

Gently fry the onion in the oil, until it is soft but not brown. Dissolve the miso paste in hot water and add it to the onions. Take the whisk and add the rice flour, stirring vigorously all the time. Finally add the ginger.

Leave it to simmer very gently over a low fire for forty-five minutes and serve this sauce hot with the toasted almond dish.

Hazelnut Sauce

50g (2 oz.) hazelnut paste
½ cupful water
the juice of ½ lemon
honey to taste

Cream the hazelnut paste and the water until it becomes light and smooth. Add the juice of half a lemon and some honey to taste. Stir well and add a little more water if the sauce has become too thick.

This sauce goes well with a bowl of wheat germ, cornflakes or oatflakes. Also good with a fresh fruit salad, though a little extra lemon juice is usually added for this purpose.

If the fruit in the fruit salad is sweet, the lemon juice in the sauce is essential. If the fruits are quite sour, the sauce can be used as it is.

19

Miscellaneous Ideas

Quick Cheese Sauce
This is a sauce for beginners or for cooks in a hurry, who want to put a meal on the table in very little time.
This sauce has one distinct advantage: it cannot go wrong!
   You will need:

150g (5 oz.) cheese-spread
3 dcl (10½ fl. oz.) milk

Bring the milk to the boil in a heavy saucepan. Add the cheese, stirring all the time. The cheese will soon melt, go on stirring until the sauce becomes smooth and thick.
   Serve it hot with boiled potatoes or rice or with boiled endive or chicory. Some chopped-up parsley or chives makes the sauce a little different, perhaps a little more interesting.

Tempura or Fried Vegetables
All vegetables that can be cut to cubes or slices are suitable for this kind of preparation.

Take:

1 part wholemeal or buckwheat flour
1½ parts water

Make it into a batter.

Dip each cube or slice of vegetable into the batter and fry it in oil. The tempura is cooked, when it is golden-brown.

Place the cooked tempura on a piece of kitchen paper to drain off the excess oil.

Serve hot with dry, cooked grain dishes or with mashed potatoes.

Fried Cheese Slices

4 large slices of cheese of 50g (2 oz.) each
25g (1 oz.) wholemeal flour
2½ tablespoonsful water
breadcrumbs
oil for frying

Make a smooth mixture of the flour and the water.

Dip the cheese slices into this batter, coat them with breadcrumbs and fry them quickly in very hot oil.

Do not prick, as the cheese will run out of the crisp outer shell.

Serve immediately.

Berberry (or Berberis) Jelly

Armed with good gardening gloves the berries of the berberis shrub can be picked. It has many sharp thorns, so be careful.

Pick as many of the oblong berries as you can. Wash them thoroughly and cook them in a little water for five minutes. Pass them through a horsehair sieve. Add half the weight of the berries in sugar, pour the mixture into clean jam jars and leave it to set. Berberries set very easily, hence the relatively small quantity of sugar.

This refreshing jelly is delicious with porridge or on toast.

Some people say that this jelly is particularly good for people who suffer from kidney or liver complaints.

Mountain Ash Berry Juice

Pick 1 kg (2 lb) ripe Mountain Ash berries. Wash the berries and
cook them with as little water as possible. Boil for five minutes and
pass them through a fine horsehair sieve.

Use 400g (1 lb) of sugar to each litre (1¾ pt.) of juice. Bring the
juice and sugar to the boil again and boil briefly. Pour the juice into
clean bottles. A delight on a winter's day as a drink or over a
pudding.

Mountain Ash berry juice is very rich in vitamins and trace minerals,
so it is very healthy as well as delicious.

20
How to Cook and Be Healthy

- Serve a milk or grain product with pulses, as this enables the body to absorb the vegetable protein of the pulses more easily.

- Always add a knob of butter or some oil to carrots to preserve the vitamin A.

- When using parsley, do not neglect the root. It tastes better than the greens and can be used in soups and sauces.

- Use the refrigerator sparingly, especially with grain products as they lose their taste.

- Try to avoid the use of vegetables and fruits that are out of season. They suffer loss of vitamins and strength in storage and transport.

- Never discard cooking or soaking water, but use it in soups and sauces. It often contains valuable trace minerals and vitamins.

- Never leave vegetables in water for a long time.

- Cut vegetables shortly before use. Otherwise too much vitamin C will get lost.

- Use all parts of the fruits and vegetables, when possible. When they have been grown on a biodynamic farm, the skins are as healthy as all other parts.

- Use salt and sugar sparingly - even though it may be brown sugar and sea salt.

- The use of cold-pressed oils is only useful when they are not heated - so never use them for frying.

- Renew the oil in the deep-frying-pan every five or six times. The oil becomes rich in polysaturated fats, through repeated heating. It becomes harmful to the blood vessels.

Index of Recipes